The Rise of UKIP

Previous page: Nigel Farage MEP in 2014

The Rise of UKIP

Bill Etheridge

with additional material by
Janet Bew & David Stepney

www.BretwaldaBooks.com
@Bretwaldabooks
bretwaldabooks.blogspot.co.uk/
Bretwalda Books on Facebook

First Published 2014
Text Copyright © Bretewalda Books 2014
Cover design by dkb creative www.dkbcreative.com/
Bill Etheridge asserts his moral rights to be regarded as the author of this book.
All rights reserved. No reproduction of any part of this publication is permitted
without the prior written permission of the publisher:
Bretwalda Books
Unit 8, Fir Tree Close, Epsom,
Surrey KT17 3LD
info@BretwaldaBooks.com
www.BretwaldaBooks.com
ISBN 978-1-909698-33-8

CONTENTS

Introduction

T his book is about the political and electoral rise of UKIP. This rise has been dramatic and filled with incidents. A white knuckle ride with more than its fair share of scares, shocks and jolts along the way. The one thing we can be sure of is that there are many more to come.

The establishment will continue to try and derail UKIP and will continue to fail. Their failure will be very easy to explain, they simply do not understand what UKIP is. The opponents of UKIP see it as a broad party of protest with a single uniting issue, the desire to leave the EU. This is a fatally flawed assessment and one that is at least five years out of date, maybe even more.

Many of the issues discussed in this book are EU based ones. That has been because they have neatly fitted around the improvements shown at each Euro election and in particular at the 2014 Euro elections and the live TV debates between Nigel Farage and Nick Clegg that preceded them.

But the EU issue is not what UKIP is about! The fact that our enemies cannot grasp that is why they spend so much time spinning lies about possible EU referendums or mythical attempts at repatriating power. The reason UKIP wants to leave the EU is simply to stop outside agencies controlling how our country is run and limiting the domestic change we can achieve.

Here is the great mystery, the shock news that has been a political conundrum for so long. The people of Britain do not agree with their masters. The reason so few of them have bothered to vote in general elections over recent years is that there has been nobody to vote for. Nobody who will stand up in a reasonable but firm way and say "I am proud of Britain and I want to retain its traditions, heritage and culture". That has now changed, at last there is an alternative to the

Social Democratic consensus that has been trashing our country and way of life for decades.

Anybody who goes out onto the streets campaigning for UKIP cannot fail to be touched by the genuine and heartfelt good wishes coming to us from people of all backgrounds, ethnicities and religions. They are desperate, truly horribly desperate for somebody to drag our country back from the brink of absolute financial and cultural disaster. The policy makers hiding away in Westminster have never walked down a street in Wolverhampton or Birmingham or many of our Midlands and Northern areas and spoken to the people there looking on in dismay at rows of boarded up shops, at groups of immigrants from eastern Europe apparently with no real purpose other than to congregate, at churches falling into disrepair and traditional pubs closing at an alarming rate. If these policy makers left Westminster and travelled out to the real world they would understand the suffering and fear that their policies are causing.

The rise of UKIP is a democratic revolution. It is the people of Britain rising up and fighting to wrestle power from the elite. The out of touch and those who comfortably don't care about anybody but themselves.

The people of Britain are slow to rouse to anger but when they are aroused no amount of platitudes, spin or electoral bribes will put out the fire.

Chapter 1

Before the Rise

The Rise of UKIP can probably be dated to 2009, but to understand the way in which UKIP has come to be the third force in British politics, it is necessary first to look back over the history of UKIP. Without a proper understanding of where UKIP has come from, it is impossible to understand where UKIP is going to. I must confess at this point that I did not join UKIP until early in 2011, so for this opening section I have relied on the memories of others and on the party records as well as newspaper cuttings and other sources.

What is known as the United Kingdom Independence Party (UKIP, or UKIP) began life in 1991 as the Anti-Federalist League. This was a cross-party campaigning group that was opposed to the Maastricht Treaty on European Union. That Maastricht Treaty transferred significant powers from the member states of the European Union (EU) to the EU itself, and significantly to the European Commission. The treaty was highly unpopular in the country as a whole, but the Conservative government of John Major was pledged to get it passed through Parliament. Given that both Labour and the LibDems supported the treaty, this seemed a foregone conclusion. There was a large minority of Conservative MPs who opposed the Treaty - Major would later famously refer to them as "bastards" - but while they could slow the Treaty down it was unlikely that they would be able to stop it. One of these "bastards", incidentally, was Christopher Gill who later became a senior member of UKIP and was - many years after the Maastricht debacle - to become my mentor.

In this atmosphere Alan Sked, a lecturer at the London School of

Economics and member of the Bruges Group, decided to take action. He declared that for all three big political parties to support a measure that the people did not want was undemocratic. The Anti Federalist League was initially started as a pressure group, but at the 1992 General Election it stood 20 candidates. All 20 got less than 5% of the vote and so lost their deposits.

In 1993 the Maastricht Treaty was passed by Parliament. Sked and other members of the Anti Federalist League met to decide their next move. They decided that they should found a political party dedicated to campaigning to take Britain out of the European Union. They decided to call it The United Kingdom Independence Party. Before long the party became known by its initials of UKIP (pronounced "you-kip") and its members were dubbed "kippers".

At this date the majority of the small number of members were formerly in of the Conservative Party. There were a few former Labour members or former Liberals (including Sked himself), but most came from the right wing of politics. Among these early members were two men who would go on to play a major role in UKIP.

The first was Gerard Batten, who had never belonged to any political party before and who worked for British Telecom. Batten was the election organizer for the 1994 European elections and was then appointed Party Secretary. He wrote the first Party Rule Book which operated for many years and he was responsible for the administration of the party membership. He held that role until 1997, but even so found time to be a tireless campaigner and candidate. Batten has fought numerous elections for the Party and would go on to be an MEP for London, party spokesman on Defence, and later Immigration and Home Affairs, and is one of the most enduringly popular leading members of UKIP.

The second figure to join as a founding member was commodities trader in the City named Nigel Farage. In June 1994 Farage stood for UKIP in the Eastleigh By-Election caused by the death of Tory MP Stephen Milligan. He got only 952 votes, 1.7% of the total, but came fourth. He later declared that the fact that he had beaten Screaming

Lord Sutch of the Monster Raving Looney Party showed that UKIP had become a proper political party in the eyes of the voting public, not a mere fringe group.

At the 1997 General Election UKIP stood 193 candidates. The party was almost entirely ignored by the media and got a fairly dismal 0.3% of the vote. This put UKIP on a par with such fringe parties as the Natural Law Party, Socialist Labour and the Alliance. On the other hand, UKIP did beat both the Greens and the British National Party, both of which were treated rather more seriously by the national media.

The Eurosceptic movement at this election was dominated by Sir James Goldsmith and his Referendum Party. Buoyed up by the funding that Goldsmith could give to it the Referendum Party fielded 547 seats and had an impressive media operation. It was largely due to Goldsmith that Labour and the Conservatives both pledged that they would not give up the £ to join the new Euro currency without first holding a referendum on the subject.

Soon after the General Election, Goldsmith died and the Referendum Party was wound up. A large proportion of its members then joined UKIP, bringing in a much-needed boost of numbers and funds.

Sked left the party at this point and a leadership election resulted in Michael Holmes becoming UKIP leader. Holmes led the party into the 1999 European Elections. He successfully positioned UKIP as being the only party opposed to the European Union and gained a fair amount of positive media coverage. The result was that UKIP got 7% of the vote and, under the complex D'Hondt system of proportional representation used in European elections, gained 3 Members of the European Parliament (MEP). These were Holmes himself, Farage and Jeffrey Titford.

The following year Holmes made a speech that proved to be his undoing. He made the point that the European Commission held the majority of power within the European Union, but it was entirely unelected. Instead, he suggested, that whatever power the EU had should be vested in the elected European Parliaments. The National

*The open-topped UKIP Battle Bus used extensively during
the 2004 European Elections*

Executive of UKIP viewed this as a sign that Holmes was "going native". There followed a series of bitter disputes that ended with the party membership forcing the resignations of both Holmes and the Executive Council.

New elections were then held that saw Jeffrey Titford elected leader of UKIP. Titford was a genial figure who had come from the Referendum Party. He got on well with almost everyone and was the ideal person to smooth over the disputes and to reunite the party. Titford successfully pulled the party together and arranged for UKIP to field 428 candidates at the 2001 General Election. This time UKIP got 1.5% of the vote, a significant improvement although it was still disappointingly tiny.

The major achievement here was to establish UKIP as the fourth largest national party, behind Labour, Conservatives and Liberal Democrats.

Feeling he had done his job, Titford stood down as party leader so that he could concentrate on being an MEP and on local campaigns in East Anglia. A leadership election saw Roger Knapman put into office. Knapman had been a surveyor before being elected as a Conservative MP. He rose to be a junior minister under Major, but resigned that position to oppose the Maastricht Treaty. In 1997 he lost his seat to Labour and almost immediately left the Conservatives to join UKIP. He had stood for UKIP at the 2001 General Election and was one of the few to retain his deposit.

Knapman oversaw a number of organisational changes, the most important of which was that UKIP transformed itself from being an

Roger Knapman, the former Conservative MP who led UKIP into the 2004 European Elections.

unincorporated association - a sort of private club - into being a private company limited by guarantee.

In the run up to the 2004 European Elections, Knapman again positioned UKIP as the only anti-EU party, going further by taking up a high profile stance against the expansion of the EU to eastern Europe and against EU workers being given free access to jobs in Britain. He attracted to UKIP some high profile defectors from other parties, the most notable of which were the film star Joan Collins and the TV chat show host and former Labour MP Robert Kilroy-Silk.

At the 2004 European Elections the issues surrounding Britain's relationship with the EU were more to the fore than ever before. Knapman proved to be a skilled performer on television and radio, while the print media gave him more space to develop UKIP themes than at any previous election. Kilroy-Silk was also loved by the

Gerard Batten concedes defeat at the count for the election to be London Mayor in 2008 after a spirited but ultimately unsuccessful campaign. This year was the low point of UKIP fortunes with a string of poor results following a number of internal disputes.

media, his smooth persona and personal charm doing much to win him a large share of media coverage.

UKIP gained 16% of the vote, up 9% on five years earlier, and won 12 seats, up from 3. This was largely at the expense of the Conservatives, who fell by 9% of the vote and 8 MEPs. Significantly this put UKIP third in terms of votes, beating the LibDems into fourth place, and equal third in terms of MEPs elected.

At UKIP national conference that autumn, Kilroy-Silk made a barnstormer of a speech that received massive applause from the audience. The media began to speculate that Kilroy-Silk would be the next leader of UKIP, something which Kilroy-Silk did nothing to oppose. However, various high ranking UKIP figures had not taken to Kilroy-Silk and there followed a number of rows and disputes that ended with Kilroy-Silk leaving the party in January 2005.

Knapman was by this point concentrating on the imminent General Election. UKIP fielded 495 candidates and got 2.2% of the votes. This was another improvement, though still the party had no MPs. In terms of votes cast, UKIP were now solidly in fourth position behind Labour, Conservatives and the LibDems. It was a good result, but many felt it was disappointing after the European Elections - which many had hoped would be a breakthrough event.

In April 2006 the newly elected Conservative Party leader, David Cameron, made an intervention that was to become notorious. Cameron was being interviewed on the radio station LBC when the subject of who donated money to the Tory Party was raised. He ducked the question and was then reminded that UKIP was promising to use the Freedom of Information Act to get the names of donors.

Cameron then responded " UKIP is sort of a bunch of fruit cakes and loonies and closet racists mostly."

UKIP MEP Nigel Farage was quick to hit back: "For Mr Cameron to resort to this combination of petty name-calling and disgraceful smears is hardly a statesmanlike approach for someone who hopes to become the next but one Prime Minister. We are a non-racist, non-sectarian party whose offence, in Mr Cameron's eyes, has been to attempt to force his party to disclose its sources of finance. We simply will not accept this type of smear being used simply to cover the Tories' blushes on a different subject, and he should apologise, not just to us, but to the 2.7 million voters who supported us in 2004. Mr Cameron needs to learn that this sort of language in the 21st century is simply unacceptable. Fruit cakes and loonies we can live with - we have a sense of humour - but we draw the line at his unfounded accusations of racism."

In the summer of 2006 Knapman announced that he would not continue as party leader after the party conference that September. In the leadership election that followed Nigel Farage emerged as victor, taking 45% of the vote among party members.

Part of Farage's platform was to move UKIP away from being a single issue party to being a fully fledged political party with aspirations for national office and a comprehensive and coherent policy platform. He also said he aimed to bring discipline to the party and to maximise UKIP's representation in local, parliamentary and other elections.

In his acceptance speech Farage declared "We've got three social democratic parties in Britain – Labour, Lib Dem and Conservative are virtually indistinguishable from each other on nearly all the main issues. You can't put a cigarette paper between them and that is why there are nine million people who don't vote now in general elections that did back in 1992."

Farage's bid to get UKIP to stand in local elections fell on deaf ears. At this date the local branches were effectively autonomous organisations that had no need to obey central instructions. The members were mostly concerned about European issues and tended to vote for one of the three big parties at local elections. In 2007, UKIP got only 7 councillors elected.

Later that year Conservative leader David Cameron made a second bid to destroy UKIP's threat to his hold on Eurosceptic voters. This time the move was more subtle than his "fruitcakes" jibe and initially at least, it was more successful.

The big EU issue of the day was the Lisbon Treaty. This had been negotiated by the Labour government, and was opposed by

Cameron's Conservatives who were burnishing their Eurosceptic credentials. Writing in the Sun newspaper, Cameron stated:

"The final reason we must have a vote is trust. Gordon Brown talks about "new" politics. But there's nothing "new" about breaking your promises to the British public. It's classic Labour. And it is the cancer that is eating away at trust in politics. Small wonder that so many people don't believe a word politicians ever say if they break their promises so casually. If you really want to signal you're a break from the past, Prime Minister, do the right thing – give the people the referendum you promised.

"Today, I will give this cast-iron guarantee: If I become PM a Conservative government will hold a referendum on any EU treaty that emerges from these negotiations. No treaty should be ratified without consulting the British people in a referendum."

There were many in UKIP who feared - and some in the Conservatives who hoped - that this pledge would fatally undermine UKIP's appeal to Eurosceptic voters and return them to the Tory fold.

Nigel Farage gave no sign of being deterred. He just got on with his job of preparing for the 2009 European Elections.

Chapter 2

Reasons for the Rise

By the autumn of 2008, UKIP was at rock bottom. The party was being buffeted by disastrous election results, falling membership and high profile squabbles among leading members. Other politicians felt free to insult UKIP and its members with impunity. It seemed as if things could not possibly get any worse.

They couldn't.

Although UKIP appeared to be on the ropes and about to be knocked out, the fact was that the foundations for the rise of UKIP were already in place. The pieces that were to come together over the following months and years were disparate and scattered. Only a very few people saw them and even fewer could see them forming any sort of a pattern. Credit to Nigel Farage for being one of those. Some accused him of being optimistic. Maybe he was, but only as regards timing, not over the basics. The rise was to come later, but its form was pretty much as he was privately predicting at this time.

Commentators outside UKIP have generally misunderstood both the party and its appeal to voters. I must confess that at this date, I was among them. I was still in the Conservative Party in 2008 and shared the views of many Tories that UKIP was an unfortunate distraction. Conservative voters and activists were voting UKIP in small numbers to protest against the European Union and its works. I, and I think many other Conservatives, sympathised with the hostility to the EU, but believed that the Conservative Party represented a broad church of opinion on the centre right. By splitting that vote, UKIP was making a Conservative victory less likely. In fact I had missed what was really happening in Britain.

By 2008 there was a widespread, but largely suppressed feeling that Britain had taken a wrong turn. This was not an old-fashioned Right vs Left split, nor a divide between generations. Political commentators and politicians were, and are, so used to seeing things in these terms that they missed what had happened. David Cameron certainly missed it, and in that lay UKIP's great opportunity. But I am getting ahead of myself. First, let's look at the problems before we look at how politicians failed to deal with them.

I grew up in a nation that was distinctly and clearly different to the modern United Kingdom. The changes are not just the understandable differences that come with progress and the passing of time. These are fundamental changes to the national character and the society we live in.

In the 70s and 80s we had a relatively clear understanding of the strengths and weaknesses of our country. We knew that we were a pale shadow of our former glory but we still managed to retain a sense that being British was still best. The Queen's Silver Jubilee in 1977 was a national party and flag waving patriotism was the order of the day. Nobody felt self conscious about patriotism, it was normal.

The Second World War didn't seem that long ago, indeed it was still the subject of everyday conversation and a part of most comedian's repertoires. The "British Sense of Humour" was irreverent, sometimes lewd, often xenophobic and never Politically Correct. We prided ourselves that being British meant that you could take a joke; we had the ability to laugh at ourselves. It is fair to say that the humour was often overly simplistic and childish but people simply accepted that if they didn't like it, they could change channel.

People held strong political views and weren't shy about expressing them. The politicians of the day reflected this with forceful characters like Arthur Scargill, Enoch Powell, Tony Benn and of course Margaret Thatcher putting forward extremely powerful arguments on behalf of their supporters. The political sphere was vibrant and alive with conflicting ideologies battling it out. Even the Centre ground had interesting and dynamic politicians like David Owen and Roy Jenkins.

There were very clearly defined classes, including a huge, real, Working Class. These men and women worked hard in factories and were proud that they paid their own way through the fruits of their efforts. It was accepted that a working man would spend time in his local pub for a pint and a smoke before returning home for dinner.

By 2008, Britain had changed. Pubs were closing at a fantastic rate. Even those that are still open are affected by the smoking ban. The flat cap wearing working man of years gone by would have no place to spend his time today, even if he still existed in any numbers.

The manufacturing sector has virtually disappeared. Low paid workers are now more likely to be employed by shops. The working class solidarity of years gone by no longer exists.

A new group of people has emerged, people with no work ethic and no intention to get paid employment. This "underclass" lives contentedly on state benefits; pride does not enter their thoughts. Patriotism is something that is often frowned on. It has been marginalised and is now often considered the domain of extremists. An air of general cynicism pervades the whole country. Pride in being British is considered somewhat quirky. The famous British sense of humour has been censored. Comedy that could offend people is now frowned on and even censored. Laws have been passed that could conceivably see a comedian end up in jail.

Politicians are now considered to be "all the same". The gap between the parties has narrowed considerably and the senior politicians on all sides seek to present themselves in a very similar way. Their main and overriding aim is to avoid causing offence or saying anything that could lead to a heated debate. I very much doubt that the firebrands of old would be allowed anywhere near the front benches of their respective parties now.

This dramatic change to our country did not just happen over the course of time. It was not a gentle drift towards this debilitated state. In 1997 Tony Blair became Prime Minister.

Tony Blair is a fantastically talented politician. He has the ability to speak with apparent sincerity and honesty at all times. In the early days his toothy grin and honest expression had the country in its thrall.

Not only is he a talented presenter and salesman of ideas but he is superb at reading a national mood. The British people in the late 1990s were collectively ready for a change and Mr Blair seized the moment.

We were ready to become more sympathetic and understanding as a nation. We wanted to soften the rough edges of our society. The trials and tribulations of the 70s and 80s had taken their toll and we were ready for a fresh, optimistic start. The catalyst of Princess Diana's death set the scene for major change and Tony Blair realised he had an opportunity.

Mr Blair took this opportunity to embark on a major project of social engineering. This project has been highly effective, and equally disastrous for many in our country. The whole story of New Labour has been the deliberate effort to change a nation's character. I believe the final step of this change was intended to be our national surrender to the European Union and to become a colony of the new super state. It is no secret that there were behind the scenes moves to get Blair nominated as the first President of the EU.

We now live in the AB (After Blair) years, citizens of a country almost totally at odds with its history. The question we must address is do we continue down the path engineered by Blair and his allies, which must eventually lead to the total diminution of the English character and our absorbtion into a European super state? If the answer is no, then we have a huge amount of work to do to change the path we are on. We need to free ourselves to be British once more. We can be a more caring and sympathetic nation without totally abandoning our traditional characteristics of patriotism, humour and the control of our emotions in the face of adversity.

Tony Blair said "I didn't come into politics to change the Labour Party. I came into politics to change the country." He managed to achieve his ambitions in a far more dramatic way than even he could have anticipated. New Labour was an amazingly successful electoral machine, its public relations and presentation skills not only kept their metaphorical boot on Tory throats but proceeded to grind them into the dust.

The extent of that change is not often appreciated.

It was always considered bad manners to be rude to and about women or people of another race. To do so with serious intent was frowned upon when I was younger, though telling jokes that played upon stereotypes was perfectly acceptable. Now it is not just bad manners, it is illegal. Worse than that, the entire political establishment, media world and public sphere generally has been enslaved by the new politically correct elite that was put in place by Tony Blair.

Everyone involved in public life is forever looking over their shoulder, wondering what the unelected guardians of the politically correct holy grail will say or do. Before a politician opens his mouth, he no longer asks himself if what he is about to say is correct or will be good for the country. Instead he asks himself if he will be branded a racist, sexist or politically incorrect pig.

Those on the Left decry the actions of Senator McCarthy in the USA during the 1950s. He instituted hearings aimed at driving Communists and Communist-sympathisers out of government employment and positions of authority. The Left describe his actions as a witch hunt and a hideous example of bigotted intolerance. And yet in Britain today they behave in exactly the same way.

In February 2014 Donna Edmonds, a UKIP councillor in Sussex, remarked on line that the decision of a hotelier not to serve gay people, while reprehensible, ought not to be a criminal offence. She was making a point about how the free market can be a force for moral good. She pointed out that a hotel that did not serve a section of society - be it gays or people with blond hair - would do less business than one that did. Over time the hotel would do less business, be less profitable and might go out of business altogether. The free market was, she maintained, a self-correcting mechanism that in the long term would inevitably reflect the mores and morals of the wider community.

Immediately and inevitably she was accused of being on the side of racists and homophobes. The cries and accusations came loudest from the Left. Ms Edmonds was hounded by journalists demanding to know why she supported racists. She was bombarded on Twitter with accusations, threats and abuse. The virulence of the attack was driven, I think, by a desire to shout her down and close down the debate. The Left did not like their views and dominant position being challenged, so the person who dared to oppose them had to be silenced. Debating the issues did not take place. Nasty abuse and threats did.

It is not just on issues of race or gender that the Left behaves in this bullying way. Take climate change - or "global warming" as it was called before the globe stopped getting warmer.

Until 2004 David Bellamy was a popular naturalist on British tv and radio. He fronted numerous shows about wildlife and the environment. He campaigned for nature reserves and against industrial pollution. Then, in 2004, he went public with his doubts about the reality of global warming and the need for the massively expensive measures being taken to cut down on carbon output. "There are no facts linking the concentration of atmospheric carbon dioxide with imminent catastrophic global warming," he stated. Almost at once he became unemployed. Wildlife and nature trusts that had previously welcomed him as a trustee, president or spokesmen dropped him. The BBC was no longer interested in using his services. His income plummeted. The career of another TV personality, Jonny Ball, similarly went into decline when he voiced scepticism about global warming and came out in support of nuclear energy.

It was Tony Blair's government that went a long way toward institutionalising this in British society. Take the career path of lawyers, for instance.

The Bar used to be self-regulating, but New Labour changed that, creating a quango called QC Appointments. The criteria the quango imposes include a commitment to diversity. It is vital to stress that this doesn't mean having more diverse QCs – for which a good case can be made. It means promoting barristers who have a political commitment to "diversity" in the Leftist sense of the word. The quango makes this exceptionally clear. "Diversity competence," it said in an annual report "includes both awareness and action. Being aware is not enough: there must be evidence of support for the principle and practice of diversity, or personal action. The Panel sought evidence of a pro-active approach to diversity issues which in outstanding candidates ran like a consistent 'thread' through their language and behaviour."

It is obvious that any lawyer who wants to progress to be a QC must be of a left-wing bent - or at least pretend to be so. The QC Appointment quango is imposing a political test on applicants. In the name of diversity, a less diverse cohort of QCs is being created, one whose members are expected to endorse the Left-liberal orthodoxy. The lawyers are not alone, of course. Teachers, social workers, even soldiers are expected to toe the line. It sometimes seems that the main purpose of the police force is to be inclusive, with the actual business of catching criminals being all but forgotten.

The point here is that anyone who refuses to toe the Leftist, politically correct line is frozen out of job prospects and acceptance in polite society. It is no wonder that more timid souls - or those who want to earn a living to put food on the table for their family - keep quiet about any doubts they may have. It is safer to mouth the politically correct nonsense than to risk unemployment and being pilloried in the press.

It is easy, and I think correct, to blame the Blair Government for this rise in the autocratic dictatorship of the politically correct, liberal left. But the near Stalinist society we now endure has been a long time coming.

Over the past thirty years or so British society has changed massively. I doubt that anyone reading this who is over the age of forty would deny that the words we use, the things we laugh at and the general social norms of society are radically different from the 1970s. An easy way of proving this would be to cast our minds back and think of what was considered acceptable humour in the past and compare it to now. Jim Davidson and Bernard Manning were among the top "stand up" comics; their material to a modern eye would often appear crude, xenophobic, sexist and racist. Contrast them to their modern equivalents for example Frankie Boyle and Eddie Izzard. The modern comedians are still often quite crude but their targets have changed. They are now highly unlikely to ridicule foreigners or women. Now the acceptable targets include the white working class, Americans and Conservatives. Frankie Boyle famously did a routine where he spoke about how happy he would be when Lady Thatcher died; he is not alone amongst his contemporaries in making these kinds of remarks.

Other changes are all around us. Many councils run a "Black history month" and later in the year a "Romany Gypsy and traveller history month" These Politically correct projects are no longer deemed worthy of a headline. Most large organisations now refer to sections of the community as "the BME community" The Black and Minority Ethnic community, the use of BME as a term is classic Politically Correct grouping and has become a standard term in use.

The lack of principle, both political and personal in the main political parties has become striking in recent times. The whole framework of politics and governance seems to be planned around a presentation driven desire not to offend and to be meticulously politically correct. This has led to a lack of real opposition to the general drive of politics over the past two decades. It has been considered unacceptable to criticise the levels of immigration and the principle of multiculturalism. Anybody opposing the idea of a multicultural Britain has been flirting with the classification of Racist then shown the example of the demonization of Enoch Powell as to what can happen if you speak too strongly on the matter.

Political Correctness is a philosophy that encourages us to look at groups of people as either perpetrators or victims. It looks at the disabled, ethnic minorities, women and the Gay community as victims who need to be helped and encouraged. On the other hand, smokers, drivers, Christians and white males have a hell of a lot to answer for and should feel guilt for the hand they have been dealt in life. These people should accept regulation and heavy taxation as their just desserts while the full power of the state should be thrown behind supporting the victim groups. This philosophy allows for a situation where motorists are little better than ozone destroying villains, murdering the planet with the dreadful emissions from their vehicles.

The motorist is subject to a huge amount of regulation and laws designed to criminlaisehim whilst at the same time paying a vast amount of tax every time they visit the petrol pumps.

The BBC is the great bastion of Political Correctness in our country. Indeed Michael Buerck recently accused it of having a "creed "of PC. Whilst Andrew Marr accused it of having a "cultural liberal bias". It is not only senior BBC journalists who have admitted to this. Former business editor Jeff Randall was quoted in 2006 as saying "the BBC is not neutral in multiculturalism it believes in and promotes it". The BBC annual accounts in 2009/10 detailed a budget of £4.26 Billion, so it seems that the proponents of PC have a massively powerful ally.

This authoritarian nightmare has been growing ever more powerful with every year that passes. The lesson of history is that the British people are very slow to anger and it normally takes a particularly obvious threat to move them to action. A gradual diet of regulation of our actions, coupled with an environment where it has become fashionable to be critical of our history and disapprove of people who are determined to improve themselves has gradually changed our society. Why should people be mugs and go out to work hard at jobs that command little "respect" when they can stay at home living on generous benefits whilst allowing immigrants to flood into the country and do the work that large numbers of the British "wouldn't get out of bed for".

Andrew Neather, a former advisor to Tony Blair admitted in 2009 that the record breaking mass immigration of the Labour years was part of a plan and there was "a driving political purpose" behind the policy. The aim was social engineering on a grand scale. While this engineering was going on, the British people refused to take up the jobs that were luring the immigrants in whilst privately grumbling about the number of foreign voices and unusual buildings including Mosques and Temples popping up around them.

The fact is immigration is not necessarily a bad thing and our nation has benefitted throughout the centuries from influxes of new ideas and people from abroad. The favourite food of most Britain's is now curry according to the Telegraph newspaper in July 2011 and I include myself in this. The important factor in immigration should be that the immigrants are encouraged to mix in with the existing population so that everyone can be enriched by the experience. Multiculturalism does the opposite to this and encourages the growth of ghettoised areas like the ones we see in parts of Birmingham, Wolverhampton and Manchester.

Many people, myself included, expected that the main political party of the right of centre - the Conservatives - would stand up against this insidious, unwanted rise of politically correct dictatorship. We found instead that under David Cameron the Conservatives have caved in. Worse, the Conservative Party has become a cheerleader for the sort of politically correct nonsense that so many people oppose and which is so inconsistent with traditional English characteristics.

Throughout the long years of New Labour, people were willing to put up with it. The economy was booming and it is easy to push concerns and worries to the back of your mind when you have a well paid job and your children seem assured of a prosperous future.

Then came the credit crunch of 2008 and the following recession, together with the economic turmoil since. This has destabilised things. What people might have put up with in the good times, they would no longer tolerate in bad times. People began to ask questions as to why our industry has declined, why we have generations of kids with no competitive ethos and countless people whose families have not worked for generations. Economic realities are causing Government to reach for their calculators and realise we can no longer afford to live in the artificial, unreal construct of politically correct over-regulated Britain.

Turning to the world of politics, we can see where this can lead by looking at David Cameron. In February 2006 he declared "Issues that once divided Conservatives from Liberal Democrats are now issues where we both agree. Our attitude to devolution and localisation of power. Iraq. The environment. I'm a liberal Conservative."

The pervasive influence of Political Correctness in the

Conservative party seems to have begun under Michael Howard, but came to the fore under David Cameron. In the run up to the 2010 General Election I saw this at first hand due to my then involvement with Dudley North constituency Conservative party. Due to personal problems, the candidate initially selected for the area had been dropped by the party and with an election looking imminent it was decided that we must select a new candidate with some urgency. The Conservative Party has long had a policy of only allowing candidates to be selected who have already been through an interview at head office. In Dudley we would have preferred somebody local, but there was nobody to hand who had been through the central process and there was no time for anyone to have a go. We decided to plough ahead and try to choose as strong a candidate as possible.

The vacancy was advertised to those who had been approved by the central interview system. Those interested sent in their CVs and we whittled them down to a list of twelve candidates that the committee felt would be worthy of interview. Unfortunately this list was rejected by Conservative head office on the grounds that there was not a fifty fifty split between male and female. After the list was rejigged to reflect the priorities of Tory high command, the twelve candidates were contacted and asked to attend an interview at the Dormston High School in Sedgley, Dudley. The aim of this interview was for the list to be whittled down once again to four. The best four would return in a few days for a final showdown to decide who the candidate would be.

The day of the interviews was absolutely fascinating, and at the end of the day a secret vote of the executive committee resulted in four candidates being chosen. The figures showed that those four had gained massively more votes than the others. Unfortunately, the party apparatchik in attendance would not allow our selection, the reason being that we had selected three men and one woman. We were forced to drop one of the men and replace him with a female candidate who had gained many fewer votes. This was, I thought, unfair both on the man who had been dropped and on the woman who was promoted. He obviously lost out on the chance of becoming candidate, while she then had a totally futile and pointless journey up from London a few days later for a selection vote that she had no chance of winning.

At the end of the process we did end up selecting a very strong, male candidate but this was almost despite the efforts of the people running the party. As a person who first became interested in politics because of his admiration for Lady Thatcher, I did not feel I was in any way biased against women, I simply wanted to select the best candidates regardless of gender.

All these shenanigans were down to an obsession by the central party that we had to be seen to be inclusive of women. The final result was not affected - we ended up with the chap we would probably have chosen anyway, but it all left a nasty taste in the mouth. We were supposed to be choosing the person best placed to represent the Party at an election and, we hoped, to represent the people of Dudley North in Parliament. Instead the entire process was hijacked in a futile effort to show that the Tory Party was obsessed by inclusivity and gender balance - in other words that it had become part of the new Leftist establishment.

Things were only going to get worse. Dudley North is a classic Black Country area with a famous background of heavy industry and many of the problems associated with the decline of those industries. It soon became clear that the classic old fashioned conservative concerns of law and order, "benefit scroungers" and immigration were very much top of the list of concerns. I felt that these should be good topics for our campaign in the area to focus on. I was therefore rather surprised to find all of this feedback ignored in favour of following advice from head office focus groups. We were definitely not to focus on immigration, instead it was important we get the message across that we loved the NHS, an odd thing to do in my opinion as I could not see how this made us any different to any other party.

I later understood that this was all part of the process known as "Detoxifying the Brand". As the campaign went on, the time allocated for speaking to people got less and less to be replaced by spending whole days at a time delivering glossy leaflets focussing on pictures of David Cameron with NHS staff and personality pieces about our candidate emphasising what a nice chap he was, which indeed was true.

The Conservative party under David Cameron has followed the lead of Labour under Tony Blair and removed politics and debate from the makeup of political parties. Indeed I was told by a senior Conservative in the Midlands area that I had to understand that "Conservative policy is not the same as conservative principle".

By 2008 this had caused a widespread disillusionment on the Right that was to gain in force over the following years. At national levels the main three parties were pursuing policies that were so broadly similar it was very difficult for anyone to whip up any real passion in an election. The declining voting figures show that the public is tired of making choices between parties that seem to be no different. This is starkly shown by the decline in turnout from the high of 83.9% in 1950 to the disappointing figure of 65.1% in 2010. It is not just the blandness of politicians that is to blame for the decline in voter turn out. The people of Britain are not stupid. They know that many powers that used to rest with our Parliament in Westminster are now held by the EU in Brussels. No matter who we vote for in our elections, the people who hold the real power will not change. If there is no point in voting, there should be no surprise that people stop doing it.

Not only do the policies of the main parties seem remarkably similar but the leadership is also uncannily alike. The tendency is for the leading politicians of our age to have been to public school then studied Politics, Philosophy and Economics at a leading university. From there they go on to work on the staff of a senior politician before emerging from their apprenticeship to steadily move up the front bench ladder. There are, of course, some politicians who haven't followed this route but they are finding it harder and harder to climb the ladder. Indeed it is almost impossible for aspiring politicians who do not fit the mould to actually get onto the ladder in the first place due to the requirement that candidates have to beapproved by head office before actually being allowed to apply for positions.

Lower on the ladder, at local Council level, it is getting harder and harder for individuals with any strong personal opinions to get a chance in winnable wards with any of the established three parties. This leads to an infrastructure of 'yes' men and women. There seem to be very few local Councillors with any real political principles, although there are obviously some very notable exceptions.

The thrust for British politics since 1991 appears to have been more about gradually managing a hand over of power to Europe than about governing the country in a way representative of the electorate's opinions and views.

As a nation we have strayed so far from genuine democracy that the way back is going to take a tremendous effort, and may not even be possible. The rules and regulations that we live by coupled with the intangible presence of Political Correctness, mean that we no longer have the freedom of speech to effectively fight back without a struggle.

Trapped in the 'Westminster Bubble', the majority of MPs, and even more senior political figures, simply could not see the problem. They spoke to each other in politically correct banalities, congratulated each other on speeches filled with polished phrases and references to lefty shibboleths and basked in the coverage they got on the BBC and in the Guardian. It had become a self-centred, self-absorbed, self-perpetuating circle of mutual congratulation when it should have been an open-minded, outward looking process seeking to do the best for Britain and for the British people.

Out in the real world there were a great many people who were waking up to the reality that Britain was no longer free. The letters pages of local newspapers became full of angry outbursts from people kicking against the new establishment and the internet buzzed with literally thousands of new postings every day. People from all sides of the traditional political spectrum started to realise that there is something very dramatically wrong.

Small, young political parties sprang up to offer the electorate something different from the established big three consensus. These parties came in many shapes and sizes. In some areas, residents associations began running candidates for local elections. Elsewhere, independents began to have success. These were a very mixed bunch indeed, but what they all had in common were genuine local roots combined with a determination to get local grievances and priorities higher up a political agenda increasingly dictated from London. Outside the organised political parties, the opportunities for organised protest and resistance to the Westminster elite are growing due to a mixture of being savvy with new media and public appetite for an opportunity to get their views into the public sphere. When our elected representatives fail or deliberately refuse to express our views, the people must eventually find ways of shouting those views from the rooftops. The traditional Left have taken to the streets with increasing regularity in recent years to protest against matters ranging from the war in Iraq to the cuts programme introduced by the coalition government. The Right have expressed themselves with large internet campaigns petitioning for a return of the death penalty and a referendum on EU membership amongst other things. One notable protest against the state was organised by a mixture of traditional and modern means. I was involved in an event that became affectionately known as the battle of Stony Stratford - more on this later.

On a more national scale there were three political parties that stood outside the Westminster Bubble, but which had at least some form of national organisation and profile. These were UKIP, the British National Party (BNP) and the Green Party. All three saw victories in local government elections and enjoyed a growing membership and support. Whilst these parties had dramatically different agendas, they were proof that there was a growing public appetite for genuine change. They were clearly handicapped by a lack of finance and perhaps even more importantly the lack of a "tribal" voting base but all the same they were still making headway.

The Greens, of course, were to a great extent tied into the liberal left agenda that many felt was causing the problems in the first place. The BNP, while it enjoyed a certain amount of electoral success for a while has always been tainted by its links to authoritarian government. For a while the BNP appeared to be moderating its stance on some of its more extreme or unusual policies, but by 2008 that process appeared to have ended. Any hope the BNP had of capitalising on the groundswell of disengagement and disillusionment was fading.

Before looking at UKIP's appeal, it is worth looking at what has been termed "the Wider Conservative Family". This refers to organisations outside the Conservative Party, and therefore free of its leadership's strictures, but which reflect a generally small "c" conservatism.

I myself went on a journey through this family as my personal disillusionment with Cameron's Conservatives grew. Frustrated at lack of discussion of politics in Conservative association meetings, I decided to get involved with organisations that actively promoted discussion and radical political thought.

The first of these was the Bruges Group. This is an organisation that has become the foremost think tank and pressure group applying pressure for Britain to leave the European Union. The Bruges group is named after the famous speech made by Mrs Thatcher in Bruges where she proclaimed "We have not successfully rolled back the frontiers of the state in Britain, only to see them re-imposed at a European level".

The Group aims to promote discussion on the European Union and to advance the education of the public on European affairs. The Bruges Group's research also explores alternative international relationships and policies. Equipping politicians, key opinion-formers and the media with the information needed for a complete restructuring of Britain's relationship with other European countries.

Through the offices of these people, an opportunity was facilitated for me to meet one of the most towering figures of modern history. We had already attended one reception held by the group in Westminster. The receptions were held in a splendid house just around the corner from Buckingham Palace. Fine food and drink were served and the whole atmosphere was one of being involved with very serious "movers and shakers". Despite that, we had remarked that we were treated with more courtesy and respect by these people than we had ever felt in our local association.

When the opportunity arose to meet Lady Thatcher at a Bruges group reception hosted by the impressive Barry Legg (MP for Milton Keynes while Mrs Thatcher was Prime Minister) my wife and I were determined not to miss out. We were amongst the first to book our tickets and the feeling of excitement in advance of the event was like that of a small child waiting for Christmas morning. When the day arrived, we had a minor panic when our train was delayed on the way down, making us a few minutes late for the event. The building was absolutely rammed full of people, many of them familiar faces to anybody interested in politics, including several prospective Tory MPs who were due to contest seats at the 2010 election

We jostled our way through the crowd to take up a position as close as possible to where we thought the great lady might appear, although this was made more difficult due to my wife needing to use a walking stick due to suffering from fibromyalgia. I think its fair to say that we drank a few glasses of the superb red wine supplied but since we were meeting somebody that we had both only ever thought of as a legendary character, way beyond our reach I think we should be excused.

Finally the moment arrived, Barry Legg emerged into the packed main room escorting an icon, a political figure that had polarised opinion all around the world but in this room was certainly amongst admirers. Margaret Thatcher was amongst us !

I have often heard tell of the effect a famous figure has on entering a room but I had never seen or experienced anything like this. As the Lady entered, all conversation fell silent and all that could be heard was a gasp as over one hundred people collectively drew in a sharp intake of breath. It felt as if all the air had been sucked out of the room and we were left in a silent vacuum. Nobody moved or spoke and Lady Thatcher paused and gave what appeared to be a slightly nervous smile. This was my wife's finest moment. As a room full of dignitaries and politicians froze, she charged forwards and grabbed Lady Thatcher's hand. She gave a brief, perfectly enunciated speech, loud enough to be heard at the back of any room. The words were moving, she spoke of how Lady Thatcher's example of leadership and feminine strength had encouraged her to rise from a genuinely poor background on a council estate, to study as a Solicitor and go on to become a teacher. At the end of the words the room broke into spontaneous applause, the gravitas of the moment was only broken when, while still holding onto Lady Thatcher's hand Star attempted a curtsy. She was not as steady as she had been several glasses of wine earlier and it was in any case no easy task with a walking stick in one hand. She very nearly dragged the grand old lady to the ground ! Afterwards when they were both on steadier footing Lady Thatcher told Star how pleased she was to have inspired her in that way. There was no doubting the sincerity of her words.

This was one of Lady Thatcher's last public appearances before ill health forced her to entirely withdraw from public life. I managed to shake the lady's hand and say a few words to her but I will always regret that due to the noise of the crowd now surrounding her, I did not hear her response. In fact after the initial ice breaking moment of Star's introductory comments the event had turned into something of a scrum. At one point I found myself rather unsubtly elbowing someone out of my way as he tried to interrupt my moment with the great lady, only later did I realise it had been former Chancellor Lord Lamont !

Stuart Wheeler the former Tory donor (who had recently moved over to UKIP) at the time gave the speech of thanks to Lady Thatcher. During the speech he made reference to his support for UKIP and I could not help but comment quite loudly that Lady Thatcher was a Tory. I couldn't understand why the gentleman to the side of me appeared so annoyed until I realised it was Lord Pearson, leader of UKIP at the time. Later in the speech, Mr Wheeler commented that he wished Lady Thatcher were twenty years younger, to which he received a superb repost. She managed to give us a flash back to her great years when she said, "If I were twenty years younger I wouldn't be here with you !" Classic Thatcher humour and a magic moment.

I mention these memories to show what being involved in politics should be about - and what it had been about in the Conservative Party until about 2003 or so. It should be about discussing ideas, debating politely with those who disagree with you and enjoying social events with like-minded people. It should be fun and productive. This event at the Bruges Group showed me how things had changed and what I had been missing.

I also joined The Freedom Association: While the Bruges Group always provided an excellent event with great speakers, I felt that I was really a part of the action with The Freedom Association. This organisation was set up in 1975 as a reaction against the power of the Soviet Union and the spread of socialism and trades union power in the UK.

Amongst its founders were Ross and Norris McWhirter of Guinness Book of Records fame. The values propounded by the TFA include: individual freedom of speech and choice as well as withdrawal from the EU. The Freedom Association is a non-partisan, centre-right, libertarian, pressure group. TFA believes in the freedom of the individual in all aspects of life to the greatest extent possible. They seek to challenge all erosion of civil liberties and campaign in support of individual liberty and freedom of expression.

The Seven Principles of a Free Society:

Individual Freedom

Personal and Family Responsibility

The Rule of Law

Limited Government

Free Market Economy

National Parliamentary Democracy

Strong National Defences

The TFA had grown to be a huge and influential group in the 1970s but had shrunk during the Thatcher years as there seemed no need for such a pressure group when the Prime minister was so clearly in favour of its aims. When myself and Star got involved with them the TFA was rebuilding under the leadership of its impressive director Simon Richards.

We encountered the people running the TFA at the Conservative party spring conference in Brighton. We had just crammed into a fringe meeting to hear the inspirational Daniel Hannan talk of his aim to start a British TEA party movement to emulate the dynamic force changing American politics. Dan is a fine speaker and every meeting he addresses is over subscribed. This was no exception. Myself and Star found ourselves at the back of the room unable to hear very much but with excellent access to the bar ! After leaving the event we tagged along with a group of people who had been there, it turned out that they were the TFA organisers behind the event. This was the beginning of an ongoing friendship and productive relationship which has led to us organising several speaking events in the Midlands on behalf of the TFA.

The finest moment so far with The Freedom Association was when they facilitated my meeting with my all time political hero. Yes I had already met Lady Thatcher but there was, in my mind, one person who was even more important to my political roots. Norman Tebbit, or to give him his proper title Lord Tebbit of Chingford, is a truly inspirational, heroic character. He is a self made man who had succeeded in business and as a pilot, then went on to be a massive figure in Twentieth Century politics figuring in the Thatcher governments of the 1980s. He showed great bravery and devotion to his wife in the aftermath of the Brighton bombing.

Lord Tebbit addressed a TFA event in London in 2010. Myself and Star were fortunate enough to be allowed in to the drinks reception before his speech. This enabled us to grab a few moments of conversation with him. I think its fair to say that Star was immediately won over by his charm and gentlemanly behaviour. Indeed to this day, I feel she was set a new standard which she judges me by; the Tebbit standard if you will! I was incredibly impressed by how up to date with the current thinking of "the man on the street" he was. In a brief conversation I had with him about how difficult it was to engage ordinary working class people with the messages coming from David Cameron and his Chelsea set Lord Tebbit managed to almost directly quote to me the words I had been hearing on the doorsteps. He understood that people were concerned about immigration and he also clearly saw that people going out and working hard and long hours were less than impressed with a welfare state that meant their unemployed neighbour seemed to be better off than them. Even at his great age, Lord Tebbit was still one of the sharpest politicians I had met.

Later, Lord Tebbit delivered a great speech. All of the passion and forcefulness that he is famous for poured forth in a superb speech. His description of Tony Blair and his government as the Poisoned Vine which could bring forth only bitter fruit has stayed with me ever since and is a brilliant metaphor for the disasterous Blair years.

Another, though rather smaller part of the "conservative family" is the Campaign Against Political Correctness. This organisation was set up by Conservative couple John and Laura Midgeley and boasts a parliamentary spokesman in the form of the excellent Phillip Davies MP for Shipley and scourge of the party leadership.

John and Laura are very much a London based couple and they are happy to franchise out the group to local organisers all around the country. It was a real honour to be given the title Black Country Spokesman and I decided to take the role very seriously.

I set up the Black Country Branch of the Campaign Against Political Correctness only after getting the permission of my local Conservative association, a fact that needs to be stated in the light of where my activities with this group led me. The first few meetings were held at the Sedgley Conservative club in Dudley, where we managed to attract between eight and twelve people at a time. While the people who came along were committed and interested in the subject, it was obvious that we needed more people in order to make an impact. I decided the best way to attract more people was to organise a series of well known guest speakers

Our first guest speaker was Mark Reckless MP. Mr Reckless is well known for having very clear and radical views on a range of issues including Europe. He had also made a name for himself for slightly less positive reasons by getting rather inebriated during a late night session at the Commons and thus being classed as incapable of voting. We managed to secure his services in a rather unusual fashion. We were on a visit to parliament as guests of Stourbridge MP Margot James. Star saw Mr Reckless entering a lift and instructed me to roll her wheelchair into the same lift. Once inside she rolled directly up to the MP and virtually pinned him to the wall while we nagged him to come and speak for us. In fairness to Mr Reckless I have no doubt he would have spoken anyway but Star's determination certainly sealed the deal!

After Mark Reckless, our next speaker was Phillip Davies MP. There was no need to apply any pressure. Mr Davies was only too happy to speak for us. His speech remains one of the most outstanding I have heard and his candour in the following question and answer session was remarkable and left everyone impressed.

Other outstanding speakers who have honoured us with a speech include David Campbell Bannerman MEP, Barry Legg of the Bruges Group, Simon Richards of TFA, John Strafford the pundit and author and Nigel Hastilow the journalist and author.

The toughest challenge for the Black Country branch of the Campaign Against PC turned out to be our greatest triumph to date. I had planned a major event at the Copthorne Hotel in Dudley with guest speaker Douglas Carswell MP. Mr Carswell is an inspiring speaker and radical thinker who tends to guarantee a big turnout wherever he speaks. With this in mind I had booked a larger than normal venue and paid a larger than normal deposit. Unfortunately, the planning for this event started before my departure from the Conservative party. By the time the event was due to take place I had left the party. I decided it would be courteous to write to Mr Carswell explaining what had happened and ask if he was still prepared to speak at what had been a cross party event all along. To my regret Mr Carswell informed Laura Midgeley at the Campaign Against Political Correctness headquarters in London that he felt it would be wise for him to drop out. He did not want to get caught up in a local battle between Conservatives which in his view would favour the local Labour party. I made it clear I still supported the ideas he had so eloquently laid out in his joint book with Daniel Hannan "The Plan" and wished him well for the future.

With just a few weeks to go before the Dinner was planned, I managed to switch the venue to Alex's Restaurant in Wolverhampton. The restaurant specialises in Mediterranean foods and was certainly a big change but we were very fortunate that the owner turned out to be a fine host.

With a very short while to go I had to find a guest speaker to replace Douglas Carswell. Fortunately, Nigel Hastilow agreed to step into the breech. Mr Hastilow is very much on the Right of the Conservative party and has had his own clashes with the party leadership over his well publicised admiration of Enoch Powell. He also writes a very popular column for the local Express and Star Newspaper. His speech was entertaining and great fun including a few well targeted good natured jokes at my expense.

I was very grateful to the people who rallied round to support our event, in the end we managed to sell sixty places and raise a handsome sum for the Campaign Against Political Correctness. It was touching and extremely encouraging that so many people rallied around to support us and attended the event. The local UKIP branches turned out in force but just as pleasingly, a good number of Tories attended to show their support and enjoy an extremely entertaining evening.

Invigorating, interesting and influential as these bodies might be, they alone could not solve the problems facing Britain. They were, and are, not political parties. They do not stand candidates, but instead rely on the powers of ideas to influence what is going on. By 2008 it was becoming clear that this was not enough. There was however, a great opportunity for change in this country. The people were sick of the Blairite politics we had overdosed on in recent years.

What all this added up to was that there was a wide spread and heartfelt disillusionment with party politics as it was being carried out in Britain of 2008. The three long-established political parties - Labour, Conservative and LibDems were very similar in tone, appearance and policy. They competed with each other to abide by the politically correct nostrums of the metropolitan liberal elite of London. They despised those who lived outside the M25 - with some Tories famously deriding their own rural voters as a "Turnip Taliban".

This disillusionment was not only with the Right of British politics. It also spread to the Left. Many Conservative activists disliked the EU and many Conservative voters were appalled by the politically correct stance of the party they had supported for so long. On the Left vast swathes of the traditional working classes that had voted Labour for generations were waking up to the fact that the Labour Party no longer championed their interests. It was Blair's Labour Party that had ditched policies favoured by working class families in the Black Country, in Newcastle and in Liverpool in favour of trendy concerns of fashionably left wing dinner parties held in Hampstead and Highgate. Policies to educate poor children to be able to get real jobs were sacrificed to the demands by educationalists to support fashionably inclusive teaching methods. Policies to get youngsters into starter jobs that would give them on the job training in skills that would guarantee them skilled work in later life were ditched, to be replaced by an open door immigration policy that provided the wealthy lefties with cheap builders, plumbers and gardeners and industry with cheap labour.

The BNP worked hard at subverting the Labour vote from 2004 onwards. They made a determined drive to get established in the old Labour heartlands of traditional white working class neighbourhoods. They pushed a simple message, but there was always a rather unpleasant undertow. The BNP achieved some electoral success and although that proved to be transient they did demonstrate that the Labour vote was not as solidly tribal as it had been 20 years earlier. The London-centric Labour Party bosses did not of course grasp them. They responded by shouting insults at the BNP and those who voted for it. They failed to recognise the reasons for the BNP successes, and for its failures.

The public could see only too well that we were governed by people who will say whatever it takes to gain power and then all too often totally ignore the promises they made once they achieve their personal goals.

With all three of the main parties morally and politically bankrupt the time was right for dramatic change. The opportunity was there for new leaders with fresh ideas to make a breakthrough. The question was whether the people with the necessary talents would emerge into the spotlight.

Britain was a nation ready for change. Its people craved honesty and straight talking from its leaders. They were tired of being ignored and having the values of a liberal elite thrust upon them through the media and from the rules and regulations initiated by totally out of touch politicians based in Westminster and Brussels.

It would have been easy to argue that each of us could play a part in bringing about this change. We could write letters to our MPs and newspapers, we could attend local meetings or better still set up new branches of The Freedom Association or our own versions of a British TEA party movement. We each create ripples in the status quo in an attempt to facilitate change, if enough of us make a stand for personal liberty and freedom we can make a difference, one battle at a time.

Reality intruded. Most people are too busy with their daily lives to spend the time and show the persistence necessary to effect change through this sort of grassroots action. They have children to ferry to school, football practice or ballet lessons. They have jobs to go to. They have elderly relatives to shop for. Understandably, that all takes priority over letter writing and attending meetings.

That is why political parties are necessary. People can delegate the activism needed to others, playing their part by voting at elections, joining a political party or contributing to campaigning funds.

By 2008 UKIP looked to be broken and on the way out. In fact all these factors were coming together to provide an ideal opportunity for a small party, standing outside the Westminster Bubble and endowed with commonsense policies that chimed with the disillusioned masses. The question was, 'could UKIP take advantage of the opportunity being given to it?'

Another area where the British public is regularly lied to is the European Court of Human Rights (ECHR). Our establishment masters often tell us that there is no link between the EU and the ECHR. This is patently untrue as you cannot be a member of the EU without being a member of the ECHR.

One of UKIPs most popular policies is to rip up the European

Convention on Human Rights and withdraw from the auspices of the ECHR. This would mean an end to the madness of situations like the one we had with Abu Qatada. It took many years and hundreds of thousands of pounds in legal fees to finally remove a man from our country who was openly against us and working towards our downfall. It would also save us from having to worry about crazy schemes like "Votes For Prisoners"

Our country has a very proud record of democracy and freedom. We certainly do not need foreign courts or judges ruling on our rights when the records of many of the countries they come from are at the very least questionable. The introduction and retention of the ECHR is yet another sign that the political elite have become divorced from the views of the general public. They sit around at Westminster polishing their politically correct credentials and chattering to each other, while ignoring what is going wrong in the wider country.

On a personal note I am a strong advocate of leaving the ECHR as one of my favourite UKIP policies would not be allowed while we were still controlled by it. UKIP would allow a referendum on the return of the death penalty with individual members entitled to campaign according to their conscience. I look forward to campaigning hard to restore a situation where monsters like the murderers of Lee Rigby are not suffered to live.

Chapter 3

The Rise Begins

With hindsight it was the 2009 European Elections that marked the start of the Rise of UKIP. I was a member of the Conservative Party in 2009, so I saw things from the Tory point of view - and an overwhelmingly unacceptable point of view it was, too.

When 2009 opened, we were expecting the European Election to be partly about policies regarding Britain's relationship with the EU, and partly about how Gordon Brown was doing as Labour Prime Minister. In the Conservative Party we were confident we would win the second argument as Brown was generally doing poorly and David Cameron was seen as the Prime Minister in waiting.

On the question of the EU, the Conservatives again had a strong hand. Our policies were broadly Eurosceptic and pretty robust. Best of all we had David Cameron's cast iron guarantee of a referendum on the Lisbon Treaty. It was a good story to tell on the doorsteps.

Everyone knew that the Eurosceptic vote was going to divide between UKIP and the Conservatives. The UKIP leader was Nigel Farage and every one recognised him to be an impressive performer on television and in the press. However, other aspects of UKIP were less impressive. They had a good organisation where they had members, but across great stretches of the country they had no presence at all and no ability to campaign. UKIP's performance would most likely depend almost entirely on how much exposure Farage managed to get and how well he performed.

Which all goes to show how wrong you can be.

A UKIP poster on a billboard at Exeter during the 2009 European Elections. The "Say No" slogan was used in this election, but note that the acronym "UKIP" has not yet appeared on election posters. It was thought that the phrase was not well enough known among the general public to be used in this way.

In January 2009 Harriet Harman MP, then Leader of the House of Commons in the Labour government, tabled a motion that would have exempted MPs' expenses from all Freedom of Information requests. Someone in the corridors of power decided that was wrong and leaked a vast number of expense claims made by MPs to the Daily Telegraph. The Telegraph began publishing the details in May.

At once all the issues that everyone expected the European Elections to be about were forgotten. All anyone was interested in was the scandal of the expenses claims, some of which were distinctly dodgy and others were questionable. The public were outraged, and going out campaigning rapidly became a very unpleasant experience. People shouted abuse or slammed doors in our faces.

For UKIP it was close to a disaster. Nobody wanted to talk about

Paul Nuttall MEP speaking to a meeting in 2009.

Britain's relationship with the EU - UKIP's strongest card - and since UKIP had no MPs, Nigel Farage struggled to get any media coverage at all.

Nevertheless, UKIP came out with a pretty good result. Their share of the vote crept up from 16.3% to 16.6% and the number of UKIP MEPs elected went from 12 to 13. It was not a spectacular victory, but in the circumstances it was better than had been expected.

Arguably the second most important person to Nigel Farage in the 2009 European Elections was Paul Nuttall. Paul was born in the tough Merseyside town of Bootle in 1976 and has always retained strong links to his hometown. He therefore provides a good working class balance to the home counties image of Nigel. Paul got a masters degree in British political history from the Liverpool Hope University and went on to lecture there as well as to hold other academic posts.

He joined UKIP in 2004, setting up a new branch in Bootle and recruiting an impressive number of local members. In 2005 he contested Bootle in the General Election, getting 4.1%, nearly twice the UKIP national average. He later contested local government seats in Bootle, peaking at 38% and coming second to Labour in 2008.

In September 2008 Nuttall became national Chairman of UKIP and was chosen to be the lead candidate for the party at the European Elections in the northwest. Much of the credit for the Party's success in 2009 must go to Nuttall, who was himself elected as an MEP.

Soon after the Euro Elections, Nuttall stood down as Party Chairman to become Deputy Leader. He doubled up as Head of Policy for a while, but that position was later given to Tim Aker.

Paul has always been a formidably talented organiser, and his presence in the media has been increasingly confident and effective. He is one of the few UKIP figures that the media ask for without trying to get Nigel Farage first.

Another key figure to play his part in the drive to professionalise the party has been Gawain Towler. The title that Gawain has held within UKIP's head office has varied over the years. In 2005 he was "Media Officer"; in 2007 he was "Press Officer" and since 2009 he has been "Head of Media". Before joining UKIP he was a journalist, having left the University of York in 1993 with a 2:2 in Philosophy.

His appointment as Head of Media in 2009 put him firmly in charge of our relations with the media, a not always very easy task. It is as well that Towler describes himself as being "thick-skinned", but it is his ability to keep a sense of humour that I think has made him so effective.

Certainly it was Towler who from 2009 onwards was instrumental in teaching UKIP how to handle the media. He has worked tirelessly to improve the image of UKIP in the eyes of the media, and to explain to us activists how to ensure that our actions reflect positively on UKIP.

He has also helped to get UKIP and activists on line with Facebook, Twitter and other social media. He has not been without controversy, but most of that has been in the form of the sort of fake moral outrage that the liberal left like to throw at those who challenge their dominance in British public life. In September 2013, for instance, Towler was telling UKIP activists in Manchester that they could expect several journalists to be present when Nigel Farage arrived by train and that one of them was known to be hostile to UKIP. Asked how this journalist could be recognised, Towler replied that she was "of ethnic extraction". The Guardian, predictably, blew this up to be some sort of racist scandal; but then, that is the Guardian for you.

Soon after Towler took up his new position, Steve Crowther became Party Chairman of UKIP. Steve was a well known UKIP campaigner from Devon. He stood in North Devon at the 2010 General Election and came third - one of only four UKIP candidates to achieve that. He had been born in Devon, but then moved to London where he worked for 30 years. Crowther has been close to Nigel Farage throughout, and some see the two men as a team.

Crowther's main task has been to drive forward what has become known as the professionalisation programme. This process has been largely the cause of UKIP's increasingly good performance since 2009. Without seeking to subdue the famous individuality of UKIP members, the professionalisation drive has sought to improve every aspect of party campaigning and organisation. Leaflets are to be better designed and better written. Candidates are to be given pointers on dealing with the media. Branches are to be better run. It is a far reaching programme, and an ambitious one.

Another key figure recruited in the wake of the 2009 European Elections was Lisa Duffy who took up the role of "Party Director" in 2010. I will admit that I did not have much to do with her until after the Corby By-Election (see below), though I was aware of her work. In 2007, for instance, she became head of Young Independence, the youth wing of UKIP, and did a sterling job getting that organisation sorted into good order. She set up a website for a start, something that no youth-oriented group can do without these days.

As Director, Duffy was put in charge of parliamentary by-elections. These are tricky things to organise for a by-election, especially one for the Westminster Parliament, is quite unlike other elections. It took a little time for Duffy to find her feet, but since she got into her stride at Corby, she has been unstoppable.

One event that was to prove to be highly significant came in

The author (left) with Roger Helmer MEP speaking at the public meeting held at the height of "The Battle of Stony Stratford".

November 2009. David Cameron broke his "cast iron promise" of a referendum on the Lisbon Treaty. He argued that since the treaty had already been ratified, circumstances had changed and so a referendum was not required. I went back to look over his promise. I could see no such caveat. His original promise read "If I become PM a Conservative government will hold a referendum on any EU treaty that emerges from these negotiations." There was no mention of "so long as it has not been ratified". For me, and for many others, this was when I lost trust with David Cameron and his clique.

I was not alone. Berry Legg of the Bruges Group said "What is the point in David Cameron upending one pledge on Europe, but promising he'll offer us yet more European promises in his general election manifesto? Why will they be any more credible than the 'cast-iron guarantee' he has just broken? How can David Cameron claim he'll fight to repatriate powers from Brussels when he won't even fight to implement his own past words?"

It was in 2011, having left the Conservatives and realised the limitations of the wider "Conservative Family" that I decided to join UKIP. Since then, I have been involved in several interesting and varied events. As a UKIP representative, I was invited to the University of Warwick to take part in a debate on whether or not the burka should be banned. It was clear that the invite had been sent to me with the expectation of UKIP being the bad guys in the debate. The looks of surprise on the student's faces when I set out the party's libertarian credentials was priceless. The expectation had clearly been for the "BNP in suits" lie to be the case, I was very happy to defy these expectations. I made it clear that the UKIP policy was to ask people to show their faces when in public buildings such as banks or shops but that we were not the type of party that believed in outright bans and lack of religious tolerance. I have always personally found the question of a ban on the Burka a difficult one. I appreciate the fact that people find it difficult to communicate with someone whose face is covered, whilst at the same time I would never want to stop anyone expressing their religious beliefs or their right to wear whatever they like. As far as I'm concerned people can walk down the street dressed as Spiderman as long as they show their face when interacting with other members of the public.

I have also been involved in discussions on BBC Radio several times, with frequent contributions to Radio West Midlands and Radio 5 Live. I was invited to take part in a live debate by Radio 5 Live. The ever controversial Edwina Currie had made a deliberately provocative statement about people in the UK not being genuinely poor. It had sparked enough of an outcry for the radio producers to stage a live debate in front of an invited audience. A great deal of the invited audience were Left Wing in persuasion and community workers. The meeting got extremely heated and to her credit Mrs Currie faced down several rather large and extremely angry protagonists. I was allowed to speak towards the end of the meeting and was amused to find myself booed before I had even had chance to speak. As I said later to the people involved I normally expect to be booed after I have said my piece, not before !

All of this was to prove to be a mere curtain-raiser to what became know as "The Battle Of Stony Stratford" in July 2011.

Stony Stratford is a small town in the Milton Keynes area. One of its local Councillors suggested a classic extension of the Nanny state. His proposal was that a smoking ban be extended to the streets of the town. The main justification for this being that smokers dropping their butts cause litter but there were obviously all sorts of other justifications floated. The somewhat eccentric Councillor who was behind the idea made it very clear he wanted this to be the start of a trend all across the country.

Not unsurprisingly, local people and businessmen were up in arms against the measure. They organised and began a concentrated campaign against the measure. The prime mover was a blogger going under the name of Dick Puddlecote!

The campaign culminated in a rally at a town centre pub. I was delighted to be invited along to speak on behalf of The Freedom Association. This was a classic case where the libertarian principles of the TFA were very relevant to the situation and I was pleased to get the opportunity to speak on their behalf. The other names on the bill included the maverick Conservative MEP Roger Helmer and UKIP leader Nigel Farage.

I was very much the warm up act for the more established names to follow later, indeed Mr Farage was very much later having been caught in traffic and I had left before his arrival. I had made the three hour journey by car with my wife and parents crammed in alongside me, I was glad to have the family support as a novice public speaker. It had teemed down with rain all day so I arrived rather bedraggled and soaking wet. There was a degree of confusion over when we were going to start the event as the organisers were obviously keen to await the arrival of Mr Farage, this led to a number of the natives getting restless and some at least well lubricated at the bar.

I was struck by the number of people at the event that I knew through political discussions and postings on the internet. This was a true gathering of new media activists as well as local people. Eventually the decision was taken to get the event under way and hope Mr Farage made it in time.

I was first on the bill. As I stood up to begin my speech I looked at the two hundred or so faces staring back at me in a scrum leading back to the bar, these were people who were up for some serious rebellion and wanted the Nanny State putting back in its box. I was determined not to let them down !

My speech started with a little information about The Freedom Association before launching into a full scale attack on the proposal. I ended by calling on the spirit of Churchill and asking the crowd to imagine what response the local council would have received from the great man had they told him he could not smoke his cigar in the street. With that there was a great cheer and we all raised our fingers in a V salute!

Roger Helmer followed up with a superb speech during which he promised to be back leading a campaign of civil disobedience should the measure be passed.

When Nigel Farage finally managed to arrive, he gave a typically stirring oration which made it into the media. I was sorry to have missed it.

The result of our efforts was that the measure was thrown out at the next council meeting. This may not be a massive moment in history or a front page making occurrence but it is significant. It shows that we can fight back and there are people who are prepared to make the effort to stand up for our freedoms.

In December of 2011 I was given the honour of being made the official UKIP Prospective Parliamentary Candidate for Dudley North. This constituency is likely to disappear if the coalition manages to make the planned changes in the make up of Parliament. Since this currently looks unlikely it seems that I will have the honour of standing for election to represent the area where my family and I live.

I have already touched upon the problems experienced by the Dudley Conservative Party in choosing a parliamentary candidate. Having seen how the matter was handled, or rather mishandled, by the Tories I was keen to see how UKIP did things. At first my heart sank. I found that UKIP, like the Conservatives, had a two stage process. First a person wishing to be a candidate had to get approved by a centralised selection process. I knew that by this date the Tories had introduced to their central process a requirement that any would-be candidate had to be able to demonstrate a commitment to "equality and diversity awareness". Was the UKIP process to be a similarly Stalinist procedure?

I needn't have worried. It turned out that the UKIP process was much more about ability, skills and hard work than it was about slavish adherence to fashionable London-based policies. The event took the form of a half day assessment to be held in Walsall. In order to pass, a candidate must prove himself in a series of disciplines. Firstly a test on knowledge of (but not slavish parroting of) party policy. This was very extensive and I must admit that I struggled briefly when asked the policy on fox hunting as being a townie it was not a topic that had been at the forefront of my mind! We also went through a simulated interview with a newspaper, radio station and TV station in which I fared slightly better since as I was already doing the first two quite regularly. We were tested on our ability to devise and deliver a series of short speeches on subjects picked out of a hat, a task I thoroughly enjoyed as it was quite a challenge to think on my feet. Finally we had a one on one interview with party director Lisa Duffy. At the end of the process I was delighted to learn that I was one of a relatively small number of people (thus far) who had passed.

When it came to the local party stage of the selection process; the difference with the Tory Party could not have been clearer. There was no pressure from the central party at all. Everything was left up to the local branch.

In my acceptance speech to the Dudley branch of UKIP, I stressed that while it was a great honour for me personally to be accepted as a candidate, if we were to achieve anything at all it must be as a team. Personal animosities must be cast aside and total commitment to the cause must be the order of the day if we are to win votes and ultimately seats from the other older, richer parties. To make a really

The author speaking to UKIP Party Conference in 2011.

significant breakthrough and shatter the hold of the establishment parties on British politics it is not enough to rely on the inspired oratory of Nigel Farage at a national level, it is essential we all play our part. It is not enough that we know we are right we must persuade the British public that we are right and that we are a serious, credible alternative to the discredited politicians who are ruining our country.

This new way of selecting candidates was part of the drive to make the party's efforts more professional. This desire to make UKIP more effective at gathering votes and getting our message across was really gathering pace by the second half of 2011. Nigel Farage, Paul Nuttall, Steve Crowther and Lisa Duffy had been going over recent election results, and studying the way the party had fought them. The results were instructive.

At the European Elections of 2009 UKIP had got 17% of the vote, at the 2010 General Election a mere 3.1%. Results at Parliamentary by-elections had varied from the 12.2% of the vote and 2nd position achieved at Barnsley in March to the 1% and 5th place UKIP got at Inverclyde in June. These widely varying results could, in part, be put down to the different circumstances of the elections. At Inverclyde in Scotland, for instance, the flag of non-London political outsider was waved by the Scottish National Party. The General Election was run on first past the post, which favours the big parties, the European elections were held under a form of proportional representation, which gives smaller parties more of a chance.

Nevertheless there were some consistent trends, and lessons to be learnt. Where UKIP already had a local branch, no matter how small, there was a firm base on which to launch a campaign. The local members knew what the local issues were, who the local opposition was likely to be and in which areas UKIP was most likely to get support. It was also clear that the media, be it local or national, prefer to speak to someone who is well presented, turns up on time and is reasonably articulate. And then there are such things as having somebody pick up the phone when it rings, reply to emails and collect the post now and then. This may all seems like pretty basic stuff, but UKIP is a volunteer organisation and volunteers are sometimes busy with their own business. UKIP was learning that to be a political party in modern Britain requires administrative skills as well as the right policies, attention to detail as well as an appreciation of the bigger picture.

A key test was going to be to what extent the national leadership could persuade the local volunteers of the importance of all this. The drive to increase the efficiency of UKIP was only going to happen if the local volunteers could see the point and get behind it. If the local volunteers thought that the leadership was making changes just for the sake of being bossy then the whole thing had the potential to backfire in spectacular fashion.

Leading UKIP has been likened to trying to herd cats. The coming year was going to be crucial.

Chapter 4

2012 The Year of Promise

It must be said that 2012 did not get off to a very good start for UKIP. The drive to professionalise the party had been under way for more than a year, and yet we made a classic administrative error that the media pounced on with glee.

When our agent for the London Mayoral Election was filling in the nomination papers for our candidate Laurence Webb, he accidentally wrote the campaign slogan "A Fresh Choice for London" in the box where he should have put the party name. The result was that the ballot papers showed Laurence as standing for "Fresh Choice" instead of for UKIP. Nigel Farage was duly bashed up on live TV by journalist Andrew Neil, and I am sure many voters hoping to vote for UKIP failed to put their X next to Laurence's name. Even so, our vote went up from 1.2% to 2%, not bad in the circumstances.

Elsewhere in the country UKIP avoided such slip ups in the local elections. These were held predominantly in Scotland, Wales and in English cities such as Hull, Portsmouth and Warrington. These were not good UKIP territory. Most of our activists and members were in more traditionally Conservative areas. The result was that UKIP stood relatively few candidates in these elections.

Another factor was that the professionalisation of the party structure was only just beginning. Most members by this date agreed it was necessary and were supportive, but the process was only just starting to get a grip. We were not yet either mobilised nor organised enough to stand candidates in areas where we had little strength on the ground. That would change remarkably quickly, but in May 2012 UKIP achieved very little because, to be frank, we did not try.

Monday 16th July 2012 was a night that will live long in the memory of UKIP supporters in Dudley. The date fell some time after the disappointing by-election result in Bradford West. Inside the party we knew that changes were being made that would greatly increase UKIP's ability to fight and win elections, but how far the public's attitude to UKIP was changing was more difficult to gauge.

Nigel Farage was by now fully recovered from his serious injuries sustained in the aircraft crash of May 2010. He was now out on the stump, drumming up support for UKIP across the country. At this date, the media were still focussing very much on Nigel as being the only UKIP personality worthy of featuring. Having Nigel come to a constituency was newsworthy, and so the party was using him to bolster support in areas known to be good for UKIP, and also to test the waters in areas where public attitudes were less clear.

This high profile for Nigel was something of a mixed blessing for the Party. On the plus side it meant that wherever Nigel went and whatever he did, we were guaranteed news coverage and public interest. On the other hand it put a lot of pressure on Nigel when he also had the job of leading the party in the European Parliament.

To make things doubly frustrating, UKIP's drive to modernise had resulted in an increasing number of people acquiring the skills needed to front for the party to the media. I myself was confident of being able to handle local and regional media quite well, and most other parts of the country could boast similarly trained and experienced spokespersons. On the national stage we had Paul Nuttall as an able and confident performer on television and radio.

And yet the media only ever wanted Nigel. If a UKIP story came up, the reporters wanted to talk to Nigel. If they could not get Nigel they very often refused to have any UKIP input at all. Some commentators have blamed Nigel himself for this situation. They have accused him of wanting to hog the limelight, and to make UKIP a sort of "One Man Nigel Show". This was not my experience, and talking to other UKIP activists it was not theirs either. At this time Nigel and the party were doing all they could to push other spokesmen into the media spotlight, but the media would not play ball.

The author (right) with Nigel Farage on the night of the successful public meeting in Sedgley. In addition to the poster, thousands of leaflets had been delivered to local houses.

Be that as it may, we hired the Mill Theatre in Sedgley to host a public meeting with Nigel. The foyer area was made available by UKIP organisers to other groups who wanted to share their message. Homes 4 Heroes were a significant presence spreading the word about their excellent cause and raising money through the sale of merchandise. The St John's Church Preservation Group was also in evidence sharing information regarding their ongoing struggle to save the famous Church in Kates Hill. Straits Football Academy was promoting their latest initiative to unearth the next Black Country footballing superstar. We also allowed a couple of small start up businesses to promote their efforts, including a local model!

Prior to the event UKIP members had distributed thousands of leaflets in the local area and stumped up their own money to pay for advertisements in the local press. There had been promotion on social media also, with Twitter and Face book alive with chatter about the event.

Nobody knew for sure how many people would turn up on the evening. There were estimates of 150 people but in a theatre with a 350 capacity that would have been acceptable without being impressive. On the night UKIP activists turned up early to deal with the expected - or perhaps hoped-for - crowds. To begin with there was a slow and steady flow of people in attendance, indeed the biggest triumph of the first part of the evening was to see representatives from at least some of the press breaking their own rule of meticulously ignoring anything to do with UKIP. Then it all changed.

Suddenly there were reports of parking log jams outside. On further investigation literally hundreds of people were seen streaming towards the venue from every direction. The venue was overwhelmed with the numbers, UKIP volunteers could not get around everyone with the all important raffle tickets and party information as they were simply overwhelmed with numbers. It was clear that the people of the Black Country wanted to hear what UKIP had to say. Estimates put the final number of people in attendance at full capacity for the theatre, 350.

Even better than the numbers in attendance, the sheer diversity of the crowd was a joy to behold. Men, women, youngsters, people of every different ethnicity and background streamed through the doors. Parties from local Temples mixed with representatives from local churches, army veterans mixed with college kids. This truly was an evening for everyone.

Then the time came for the speeches to begin. I took to the stage to give a brief introduction and give a little local background, the atmosphere was absolutely electric. Despite the fact I was blinded by the theatre lights and couldn't really see the audience it was obvious that an atmosphere akin to that of a Rock Concert was building up. At last the time came to introduce the leader of UKIP; I introduced

Nigel Farage who arrived on the stage to loud applause. For the next hour the crowd was spellbound by the oratory and honesty of Farage. His points about giving the British people a fair say on the EU, promoting British manufacturing, offering a fair and strong policy on immigration control and rewarding hard work were just what the people had gathered hoping to hear. At last someone was talking for them and talking well!

At the end of the evening the hundreds of people who had attended drifted away inspired and excited by what they had seen. For my part I was left with the overwhelming feeling that I had seen how good it can be. I had seen how UKIP can help to promote local businesses, how we can cooperate with important charities preserving our heritage and looking after our servicemen and I had seen how we can bring all members of the community together. You don't have to come from one particular part of the community to support UKIP, we are open to anybody who loves our country and has a passion for personal

The public throng around a street stall in Kidderminster in the summer of 2012.

liberty. Liberty and freedom to live your life and worship your God according to your own beliefs and views without an overbearing state telling you what you should be doing.

Yes the memory of Monday 16th July will live on for a very long time, certainly in my mind. Because it has proved that we can do it, we can mobilise the British public to work together and to stand up for shared values and noble causes.

My overriding emotions from the night were pride and hope. Proud to be a member of UKIP, proud to be from the Black Country and proud to be British. Hope that we can change things we can reclaim our freedom. Yes the 16th July was a great day!

I soon realised that what had happened at our meeting was typical of the reaction Nigel got right around the country when he took part in these public meetings. While the other party leaders spent the summer of 2011 joining the liberal media frenzy over the supposedly wonderful Arab Spring (and what a damp squib that turned out to be) Nigel was meeting the public face to face. Public meetings are terribly out of favour with the big three political parties of LibLabCon, but they don't half get you in touch with what people are really thinking.

From a political point of view, the autumn of 2011 seemed set to be dominated by the great non-event of the Police and Crime Commissioner elections. To be fair to the Tories, it is a good democratic idea to allow local people to elect the person who runs the local police force. That gives democratic accountability to a person who wields much local power. However, Cameron had decided that the elected commissioners were not actually going to have very much power after all. Once again, the British people were being asked to vote for a position the holder of which would have minimal power - while the person with the real power remained unelected and unaccountable. The EU system again.

Anyway, UKIP had decided not to contest the Police and Crime Commissioner elections in the West Midlands. This was due to the unpopularity of the idea and the vast cost and general difficulty of fighting an election over such a huge area with desperately limited resources.

So it would be fair to say I was not expecting the phone call I received one Sunday morning not too long before the nominations for election were due to be submitted. Nigel Farage had decided that it was important that we compete in the West Midlands area, amongst 23 others, to show that we had a strong set of domestic policies on law and order. It was clear from the conversation that somebody needed to grasp the nettle of standing in the West Midlands and that I was that person.

Obviously this was an honour and to be trusted with such a huge task by the party leader was very pleasing. On the other hand the scale of the task was huge. The West Midlands Police area is the biggest outside of London and the scale of campaigning across it was truly titanic.

The West Midlands campaign featured seven candidates with the big four political parties; Conservative, Labour, UKIP and LibDems being joined by 3 independent candidates. The Independents Cath Hannon and Mike Rumble had policing backgrounds while Bishop Derek Webley had experience on the political side of policing administration.

It is well documented that the elections were very poorly covered and media and public interest was next to nothing. In many ways this was a great shame as the campaign was waged in a good spirit with some very serious and informative debate. Of all of the political debates I have been involved in these were the ones that if they had received proper coverage would have been best for democracy. There was no personal animosity, indeed friendships were formed between the candidates. While there was personal respect there was huge differences in emphasis and practical policies between the candidates. Sadly very few people ever got to see this.

Our UKIP campaign in the West Midlands was very much on a wing and a prayer. We managed to raise under £5k to support the campaign through raffles, race nights and general low level fundraising. A figure that was dwarfed by our opponents in the other major parties and was more than matched by the Independents. Unlike other areas we suffered from the fact that our sitting MEP did not

Jill Seymour, who heads up the UKIP campaign in Shropshire, out campaigning in the village of Shifnal.

make much of an effort to help with fundraising. This meant that the campaign in the West Midlands paled into insignificance compared to the campaign run further North where UKIP MEP Godfrey Bloom went all out to compete with John Prescott amongst others. Unfortunately no UKIP candidate achieved victory in these elections regardless of how much they spent.

The UKIP campaign in the West Midlands was very much a double act with me as the front man and Jill Seymour as the campaign manager. This was a partnership which would be reinstituted for the 2014 Euro Election campaign with Jill as the lead candidate supported by me and Jim Carver.

The most notable feature of the campaign was the gruelling series of hustings that the candidates were invited to. There were 14 hustings, one of which UKIP was banned from due to a concern that our answers would "cause offence" I attended each of the other hustings across the West Midlands. The hustings were inevitably organised by vested interest groups including groups concerned with LGBT rights, a womens rights group, Afro Carribean community action groups, and a mosque. I made a point of attending every hustings in order to show there was nowhere UKIP would not go and nobody who we weren't interested in talking to.

The effect was very interesting. At each event I answered questions with complete honesty and adhered closely to UKIP policy on law and order. The great thing was to see the look of shock on people's faces when they realised that UKIP policies were not only reasonable but that they also agreed with many of them. One fairly typical response was at a hustings organised by the TUC when I was approached at the end by several people saying that they had agreed with me but could not vote for me as I was in UKIP. With each one of these conversations the door was being nudged slightly further open for people to consider voting UKIP in future.

I personally learnt a great deal during this campaign. I learnt just how much political interference there is in UK policing . In many cases, politics and procedures have lead to a situation where the policing budget is swallowed up on statistics and politically correct systems monitoring diversity etc so that there is very little money left for actual police on the streets. The complexity of the systems dictating how the police run, including a proliferation of partner agencies lead to a bureaucrat's dream and a vast waste of money. Worryingly I also learnt of many areas and sections of the community where there is absolutely no trust between the police and the public. The breakdown of trust in the inner cities has not been helped.

I attended a hustings in the Handsworth area of Birmingham that was deeply concerning. The meeting was attended by about fifty people mainly of Afro-Carribean descent. Almost all of them with horror stories of poor treatment by the police. There was no solid evidence one way or the other but if even a little of what I heard that day was true it was very apparent that there was a serious breakdown in communications and trust between the community and the police. At the end of the meeting one man took me on one side and told me

UKIP's PCC candidate in Hampshire in 2012, Stephen West, campaigns outside a "pop up shop", that is a shop rented on a short-term lease to give the party a temporary, high-profile base in an area during an election.

that despite his previous misgivings about UKIP he would be voting for us now as we were the only ones who seemed honest and outside a system he simply did not trust.

The Labour and Conservative candidates were very keen on focussing their answers around "Partner Agencies" a term which I soon learned to equate with backdoor privatisation and QANGOs. The people attending meetings and hustings were lost in a sea of abbreviations and red tape when all they really wanted was a transparent, open, honest and robust police force protecting them from crime and ensuring criminals got tough but fair treatment.

I had the unusual experience of attending a hustings in a central

Birmingham mosque. This was the first time I have ever addressed a public meeting bare foot and perhaps more significantly the first time I have ever taken questions from behind a curtain as women were not allowed into the main area. At the end of the hustings a teenage boy approached me on the way out. He told me that he had been inspired by what I had said about UKIP and our policies and that while it would not be acceptable for him to speak openly about it he would always remember the event and follow our progress. I left smiling, thinking that there was hope for the future.

As well as attending hustings I led teams of UKIP members out on canvassing sessions around the West Midlands. The differing receptions were remarkable. When out and about in the city centres of Coventry and Birmingham there was a degree of hostility from students who seemed to have been persuaded that we were the Nazi party reincarnated. They must have missed the lesson where any politics lecturer worthy of the name would explain that libertarianism is about as far removed from Nazism and Fascism as it is possible to get. It was also noticeable in these city centres that it was not always easy to find a large number of English speaking people to talk with. Still our activists in these areas made heroic efforts to try and get the message out.

Meeting the public in Halesowen, Wolverhampton and Dudley high streets was an altogether different experience. At times it felt like a home coming and the strength of positive feeling and opinion was very moving. Indeed when I met the public on the high street of my home area of Sedgley the response was so warm I was almost moved to tears. Time and again people were coming over and thanking me and UKIP for standing up for them and for traditional values. It was an experience that answers the question people often ask "Why do you bother with politics ?"

On the final day of the campaign I set out with a group of supporters on a marathon campaigning session. We started at Wolverhampton train station at 7am and finally finished campaigning at 7pm in the evening having been to Wolverhampton, Bilston, Sedgley, Gornal, Brierley Hill and Stourbridge during the day. The highlight of the day was when my father who was still out on the streets speaking with people until the bitter end was approached by a member of the Conservative party in Stourbridge who informed him he was wasting his time campaigning for UKIP because the candidate was certifiably insane as was his family. That story was enough to put a smile on our faces on the way home.

The count was an extremely nerve wracking experience. Not because we felt there was any chance of victory but because when the first ballot boxes for Birmingham started coming out we felt there was a very serious chance of losing our deposit. I certainly didn't fancy being the UKIP candidate who had to phone up Nigel Farage and tell him we had been beaten into last place and lost our deposit. The deposit for these elections had been set at £5,000 - a massive increase on the £500 deposit at parliamentary elections and the no deposit at all needed for local council elections.

It was painfully obvious as the votes from each region were announced that not only had we failed to make any headway in the cities but the fact there were 3 independent candidates had hurt us badly with Cath Hannon doing extremely well and achieving a very strong 3rd place. The only real positives were very strong results in the Black Country where they had obviously voted on the basis I was one of their own and the fact that we had beaten the Lib Dems.

On the 16th November 2012 the results of the West Midlands Police and Crime Commissioner Campaign were announced.

Matt Bennett (Con)	44,130
Bill Etheridge (UKIP)	17,563
Cath Hannon (Ind)	30,778
Bob Jones (Lab)	100,130
Ayoub Khan (Lib Dem)	15,413
Mike Rumble (Ind)	12,882
Derek Webley (Ind)	17,488
Turnout	12.31%
Rejected	7,063

UKIP Polled 17,563 votes achieving 4th place and 7.4% of the vote.

As was becoming standard practice in UKIP by 2012, candidates and key activists were encouraged to get down in writing what they felt had been successful and what had not during an election. This was yet another aspect of the drive to move UKIP away from the old practice of muddling through and instead to make the party a thoroughly 21st Century organisation. All part of the process of routine, back room hard slog that lies behind the rise of the party. Set out below are the notes I made at the time. They reveal a lot about how UKIP was campaigning in 2012 and how far the party had come since the days of 2008.

Police and Crime Commissioner Elections, Nov 2012 Campaign Report

The bald voting figures are only the beginning of the story of the campaign. I intend to give a detailed analysis of what we did well and what we did badly during the campaign.

In an election, anything less than first is losing so we need to start the work now to make sure we start winning.

The Campaign

From the outset it was acknowledged that the campaign was not going to be an easy one. We had several key factors to address:

1- Mobilising the membership. In order to cover the vast areas of the West Midlands that this campaign would be fought over we needed to mobilise the full party membership.

2 - Finance. The branches within the West Midlands and most of the membership are not wealthy. There was an urgent need to raise a fighting fund as quickly as possible.

3 – Media coverage. We needed to get media coverage in order to try and get our message out across such a huge area. This required coverage in Newspapers, Radio, TV and Social media i.e. Twitter and Facebook.

4 –UKIP Policy. We needed to persuade the electorate that the issues under consideration were ones that could be addressed by UKIP policy. The major obstacle to overcome was the perception of UKIP as a one issue party.

5 – Ambassadorship. This campaign was a wonderful opportunity to take the UKIP message to places where it would never usually be heard. A chance to show people we are a credible party with serious alternative policies and an inclusive approach.

Mobilising The Membership

The first step was to set up a team and to establish key contacts across the West Midlands. I approached Jill Seymour to act as my Campaign Manager and Agent. Her experience both within the party and of fighting elections was invaluable during the campaign. Her loss from the campaign during the latter stages to recover from an operation on her leg was an unfortunate event and she was missed.

My wife, Star Etheridge took control of the Social Media side of the campaign as well as being actively involved in much of the administration.

Derek Bennett the Regional Organiser for the West Midlands played an important part, spreading communication of our activities and helping us to liaise with the branches.

Craig Winyard offered advice and support in terms of handling the media.

Each of the branch chairmen across the West Midlands played their part with mobilising activists and raising funds. Special mention to Telford and Wyre Forest branches who, although they were officially outside of the WMP area still contributed time and money. Across the West Midlands we had teams of members and volunteers in Birmingham, Coventry, Walsall, Wolverhampton and Dudley Borough. While these teams were often small the people involved worked extremely hard.

Mike Lynch, Chairman of the West Midlands region was a constant source of strength and help who always made it clear that the efforts of our team had his support.

It is fair to say that we had a very committed and hard working team on this campaign. Without the combined efforts of the membership and outside volunteers we would have had absolutely no chance of fighting this campaign.

Finances

One of the major difficulties with fighting a campaign on this scale is the cost. While we had the deposit paid by the party the actual financing of the campaign was up to us.

We raised money in the following ways:

1 – Visits to Branches where we asked for contributions of however much the branch and its membership could afford.

2 – Individual donations. We were fortunate to receive several generous individual donations notably from Brian Seymour, Christopher Gill, Neil Hamilton and Craig Winyard amongst several others who donated smaller amounts which were all very much appreciated.

3 – Donations through the Website. We had several donations through my website.

4 – Fund raising event. The Dudley Branch organised a fund raising event which raised over £200 for the cause.

5 – Raffle held at party conference. Jill, Star, Tom Hoof and Stewart Parr all took shifts on my stall at the party conference and sold raffle tickets to the membership.

At the end of all of our efforts the campaign has a fighting fund of approximately £2,600. An amount that we worked very hard to achieve but must be recognised as incredibly small in terms of the size of the task ahead of us.

Media Coverage

In order to fight an election of this size it was important to use all forms of media to get the message out.

1 – Newspapers. We had mixed success with newspapers. The Midland Newsgroup that publishes the Dudley and Stourbridge News is viewed as being anti-UKIP. They worked hard to promote negative publicity at the start of the campaign. More positive coverage was achieved in the Express & Star, Coventry Telegraph and Birmingham Post with quotes from me being used in stories about crime and victims in the area.

2 – Radio. BBC Radio West Midlands invited me on air several times with the Adrian Goldberg programme being a regular port of call. I was also interviewed on BBC Radio Coventry, Heart FM and Newstyle Radio (an Afro Caribbean Station based in Birmingham).

3 – Social Media. We used Facebook and Twitter to spread the word about our policies and direct people to the website. By the end of the election campaign the website had received over 30k hits.

4 – TV. Clips of me at various hustings were regularly shown on BBC. I also participated in a live debate with the other candidates on the BBC news channel. I also took part in a 90 minute live debate on Sangat TV, a heavily subscribed to Sikh TV Channel.

5 – Live Web Streaming. Several of the hustings I was involved in were streamed live across the web to a larger audience tuning in via their internet connections.

UKIP Policy

This campaign was a golden opportunity to show that UKIP is a fully fledged party with a full range of policies and is not just a single issue anti-EU pressure group as we are often labelled.

As always, the party allowed candidates a certain degree of leeway once policy guidelines were established. Our West Midlands campaign was based around the following policies:

1 – Putting the rights of the victim ahead of those of the criminal. This was a national policy which is really more of an

*The author campaigning with Neil and Christine Hamilton (left)
and others on a chilly afternoon during the PCC campaign of 2012.*

indication of an attitude towards policing than a specific policy.
We believe that the public is sick of criminals seeming to have
their rights allowed more consideration than the law abiding
majority.

2 – More Bobbies on the beat. We wanted to bring back this
style of policing where the local Bobby was a trusted member
of the community often seen walking the beat in his area.

3 – No privatisation of the police. Whilst appreciating the
value of private competition in most areas of the economy and
society we believe that the police are one area where there
should be public ownership and a force accountable to the
people not shareholders.

4 –Zero Tolerance Policing in Crime Hot Spots. A rolling

programme of constantly changing and shifting Zero Tolerance Zones targeting criminals and gangs in specified crime hotspots for a limited period.

5 – Act as an advocate for the public. The Police Commissioner should act as a voice for the public demanding tougher, fairer sentences.

Ambassadorship

Those of us who spend time campaigning for UKIP know that we spend a large amount of our time trying to dispel false accusations about us, our characters and our policies. The old label of BNP in suits has been a difficult tag to shift.

This campaign gave the opportunity for me to act as an ambassador for the party and show that we are an open and inclusive party which does not tolerate or condone prejudice of any sort.

During the course of the campaign I attended a series of

My main election leaflet from the PCC elections of 2012

public meetings and hustings all across the West Midlands. I attended UKIP organised public meetings in Walsall, Shirley (with Neil and Christine Hamilton) and Upper Gornal but the majority of the events were organised by community groups.

Amongst the hustings I attended there were events arranged by the following groups in the areas listed here;

The Northfield Mosque in Birmingham

Kashmiri Association in Small Heath

The Polish Community in Walsall

LGBT Group in Birmingham

Afro Caribbean Community in Aston

Residents associations in Moseley, Birmingham City centre and Handsworth

Women's Voices Group in Coventry

Dialogue Society in Birmingham

TUC in Birmingham

Chamber of Commerce in Birmingham

St John's Church Preservation Group

In all I attended 3 public meetings and 13 hustings events. Along the way I made new friends and took the UKIP message to places it had never been before. Hopefully I played a small part in laying the groundwork for other party members to continue with our efforts to encourage a wider range of the electorate to consider voting for us and joining us

Meeting The People

There were several very successful campaign events where I went out onto the streets of town and city centres accompanied by volunteers. We went to Wolverhampton, Halesowen, Dudley, Coventry, Shirley and on a very busy final day of campaigning visited Wolverhampton, Bilston, Sedgley, Gornal, Brierley Hill and Stourbridge.

These events were extremely effective in engaging with the public and explaining our message. An excellent suggestion from Michael Wrench of Wyre Forest UKIP was to campaign at train stations handing out leaflets to the commuters. We reached hundreds of people per hour by having two sessions outside Wolverhampton train station.

Special credit needs to go to Lucy Bostick who travelled up from Essex to help on our Wolverhampton action day and Neil and Christine Hamilton who helped in Shirley

These days meeting the public were very powerful campaigning sessions and in my opinion are what politics is all about. Meeting and talking to the voting public showed them that we were in touch and decent people keen to listen to the comments and needs of the public

In Conclusion

We have learnt a great deal from this campaign and hopefully the public has learnt a little about us.

It has been proved that there is an opportunity for us to engage with the electorate as a whole and nowhere should be out of bounds for us as a party. If we approach people with humility and respect they are likely to allow us an opportunity to speak with them and possibly persuade them to our cause.

The results of the election are also worthy of analysis. They show that from a high point of 18.5% in Dudley North our results across the area suffered and fell as low as below 5% in parts of Birmingham. This is no reflection on our activists in any of the areas where we did badly; moreover it is a sign that they need our help to add to the incredibly hard work they already contribute to the cause.

We have a situation where a handful of very dedicated activists are stretched beyond their capacity trying to cover vast areas and huge numbers of people in cities like Birmingham, Coventry and Wolverhampton. To leave them without reinforcement or assistance to build their branches would be to turn our backs on vast numbers of potential voters and to leave some of our most determined activists an almost impossible task.

There is also a difficult situation in Solihull where the branch has been badly damaged by recent events involving our former MEP Ms Sinclaire. The remaining activists are very keen to try to rebuild and they helped put together a superb afternoon of campaigning when we had the visit from Neil and Christine Hamilton. Sadly the low vote that we gained from the Solihull area in this election shows that they have their work cut out to regain lost ground.

The Labour party in the West Midlands is an incredibly efficient electioneering machine. Their resounding victory in this election showed the high level of professionalism that they bring to these contests. If we are to compete with them in these large scale contests in the future we need to lay down the groundwork well in advance.

I have kept the contact details for all of the groups that I encountered during this campaign and will be forwarding them to the relevant branch chairmen. The last couple of months have given us some momentum and opened doors for us all across the region. I will be doing my best to liaise with the UKIP West Midlands Team to build on the hard work we have all contributed during this period.

We have proved that we can fight an extremely efficient and effective campaign with limited resources when we work as a team. I look forward to our teamwork continuing and important victories in the years to come.

Across the country UKIP had achieved mediocre results and not even the high spending high profile campaign waged by Godfrey Bloom in the North of England had achieved much more than give the media some interesting headlines as "Godders" and John Prescott tried to out do each other in the controversy stakes.

At a national level the campaign had been bedevilled with problems and the campaign director, Rob Burberry had his hands more than full right from the start weeding out inappropriate potential candidates and trying to magic up money for campaigns from nonexistent funds. The kindest description of UKIPs efforts both nationally and locally in this campaign would be to call it a very steep learning curve.

On the plus side, UKIP was most certainly learning. As events were very soon to show.

Chapter 5

The By-Election Surge

L ooking at things from the inside of UKIP, we knew that things were going our way. The internal drive to professionalise the party was slowly bearing fruit. We had a more coherent approach to campaigning, to building local branches and to fund raising. True this had not borne much in the way of productive fruit at the PCC elections of November 2012, but we did feel the campaigning had gone significantly better than in the General Election of 2010. I certainly thought that our efforts had been better organised and better targeted than before.

The only way, it seemed, was up. What none of us knew was that events were about to take a hand. In fact, they already had. While I was busy pounding pavements in the West Midlands others were fighting a very different sort of campaign down in Northamptonshire. It was a campaign that would confirm that the rise of UKIP was well and truly underway.

On 6 August 2012, Conservative MP Louise Mensch announced her resignation as MP for Corby and East Northants. She had won the seat for the Conservatives from Labour in the 2010 General Election. Her resignation was not a surprise as she had talked increasingly about the difficulties of combining motherhood with a political career – during an interview with the New Statesman in October 2011 she said she felt "stretched multiple ways" – but the timing of a forced by-election was something the Coalition Government would probably rather not have faced.

At first, UKIP was rather disturbed by the prospect of the campaign. By-elections are expensive things to fight. The most recent parliamentary by-election in March 2012 in Bradford West had seen us get 3.3% of the vote, down from 5.5% at Feltham in December 2011. The central party was gathering strength for the County elections of 2013, hoping to use good results then as a springboard for the far more important European Elections of 2014. An expensive by-election with an uncertain result in a constituency where we did not have a very good record was not really what was needed.

Nevertheless, political parties exist to fight elections. This was an election. UKIP would fight it.

Corby was an unusual seat. It is a marginal constituency split between the Labour stronghold of Corby and the more Conservative rural villages and towns of East Northamptonshire. It had a Conservative MP, William Powell, until 1997, when Phil Hope won the seat for Labour with a majority of 11,860. By the time of the 2005 General Election Labour's majority had shrunk to 1,517. Louise Mensch won the seat back for the Conservatives in the 2010 General Election with a majority of 1,951.

The town is staunchly Labour. Of the 30 borough councillors, 23 are Labour, four Conservative and three are Liberal Democrats. This contrasts sharply with much of the rest of the constituency. East Northamptonshire Council has 40 members, of whom 35 are Conservative and only two Labour. Oundle, for example, is a pretty market town about nine miles east of Corby and has a public school and an international arts festival. The 14 members of the town council are non-partisan but the county councillor for the town, Rupert Reichhold, is a Conservative.

UKIP had no councillors at all. However, UKIP did have a local branch which was in a position to offer local information and local expertise. I was not at the meeting that they had with the national leadership just after the by-election was called, but I gather that they were fairly optimistic of getting a reasonably good vote.

Outside Corby itself, other towns in the constituency include Raunds, which used to rely on the boot and shoe industry for employment. Now that this has disappeared, the majority of the town's inhabitants commute to work, an issue that has been addressed in the Raunds Masterplan. Irthlingborough was hit when its major employer, Dr Martens, closed its head office there when production moved to China. Snacks and baking firm Whitworths employs about 300 people.

Rural constituents have their own specific concerns, including the proliferation of wind farms. An unpopular plan to build a wind farm close to the National Trust's Lyveden New Bield, near Oundle, was turned down by the Council. The decision was overturned by the government's Planning Inspectorate, angering people who live near to the beautiful Elizabethan house. The council took the highly unusual step of joining forces with the National Trust and English Heritage to start legal proceedings against the decision, the first time a case has gone to this level, and a good indication of the public's dismay at the decision.

When news of Louise Mensch's resignation broke, Labour's candidate for the seat, Andy Sawford, lost no time in swinging into action. The son of popular former Kettering MP Phil Sawford, he is the son and grandson of Corby steelworkers. He made it clear at the start of the campaign that the Labour Party was not taking victory for granted and that they would visit as many constituents as possible and listen to every resident "taking their concerns seriously, showing that politicians can make a real difference". Andy promised he would "stand up for ordinary families whose budgets are being squeezed tighter and tighter and small companies battling to keep their heads above water, but can't get the help they need from the banks".

The fact that Labour were not entirely deaf to the underlying unease among voters came when the party's campaign literature stated: "To those who say politicians are all the same and that voting won't make a difference Andy will be a full-time MP, working as hard as he can to improve things in this area and help local people. Andy will always do what is best for Corby and East Northamptonshire - not what is best for Westminster."

The Liberal Democrats announced that Jill Hope would be their candidate on 23 August. A business manager, she announced that she had lived in Northamptonshire for more than 35 years, though it

UKIP Corby candidate Margot Parker chats to a UKIP supporter in a local bar at the end of the UKIP Action Day held in the Corby By-election on 18 August.

turned out she lived in Northampton, not in Corby. Jill Hope spoke up at the Liberal Democrats' annual conference in Brighton in September, telling delegates that she was against building more prisons. She said: "My work in Wellingborough Prison with pre-release prisoners has made me understand that people will continue to reoffend and cost us a fortune unless we provide them with the means of getting a job and becoming useful members of society. Keeping someone in prison is so expensive and this money could be so much better spent on more police officers."

UKIP introduced their candidate, Margot Parker, to voters on

August 18. A businesswoman and mother-of-two, Margot Parker lives in the constituency, in Weldon, and was a key activist in the local branch. She told voters that she believes everyone should have access to good education and that we should fight for our children's future. She said: "I've been a successful businesswoman, working in the community and building a future for my own kids. But what are we doing for the next generation? We have to fight for our children's future, before it's too late."

Her manifesto also listed rebuilding the UK's world-beating manufacturing industries, ending open-border immigration, an end to taxes for workers on the minimum wage and an end to the government propping up failed EU economies as her priorities.

Margot has had a varied career, working in, and running businesses in everything from fashion to telecoms, and got involved in politics in 2009 after becoming frustrated by the amount of anti-business regulation coming from Brussels and the government's increasing attempts to micro-manage every aspect of our lives.

She said that the biggest problem in Corby is unemployment, and also claimed to have been very vocal in her criticism of the Labour council and its handling of the building the Cube, as well as voicing concerns over the sale of land in the town to Tesco. Before the campaign UKIP had raised concern over the attempts to build a wind farm in Lyveden New Bield, and she told voters that "we must remain vigilant as the massively subsidised wind industry will certainly be back".

The Conservatives finally showed their hand on September 1, when they announced that Christine Emmett would be their candidate. Christine lives in Rutland and runs a holiday home business with her husband.

David Wickham stood for the English Democrats on a platform of saving manufacturing in the town, ending mass immigration and an immediate referendum on membership of the European Union. He was also against tuition fees and prescription charges and wanted lower taxes to stimulate growth. Relations between UKIP and the English Democrats has not always been easy. In 2004 a number of

UKIP members had left to join the English Democrats. Over the years there has been talk of a merger, acrimonious disputes and rumoured electoral pacts. Back in the dark days for UKIP of 2007 there were some who thought the English Democrats might grow to become the main right of centre rival to the Conservatives. However, the English Democrats never adopted the drive for professionalism that has been

The UKIP "pop-up shop" in Corby town centre. This tactic proved to be highly effective for UKIP, providing a high-profile focus for campaigning activity that was in daily sight of shoppers in the town centre. It has since been copied at other by-elections and at the 2014 European Elections.

adopted by UKIP. Their share of the vote and public profile has slipped consistently in recent years.

Other candidates included Adam Lotun for Democracy 2015, a new political movement started a month earlier by the founding editor of The Independent, Andreas Whittam Smith, with the idea of getting people who have had a career outside of politics to run in the 2015 General Election to try and get rid of the political class. Then there was Dr Rohen Kapur, the Young People's Party's candidate. He believed immigration from Eastern Europe was a concern for many of his constituents and admitted it was a difficult subject to tackle. Also throwing its hat into the ring was Clear, the Cannabis Law Reform party. Corby resident, Gordon Riddell, stood for the BNP having previously campaigned for election in borough and county council elections.

The United People's Party's East Midlands regional organiser, Christopher Scotton, also stood on a platform of tackling unemployment. A late entrant into the fray was David Bishop, of Nottingham, who stood for the Elvis Loves Pets party. His campaign was nearly very shortlived because on the first day of campaigning he was almost knocked over by a quad bike that was being driven at speed along the pavement.

When nominations closed on Wednesday 31 October there were a handful of other candidates including the Green Party's Jonathan Hornett and two Independents – Ian Gillman and Mr Mozzarella.

The Labour Party hit the ground running once Louise Mensch announced her resignation, wheeling in the big guns while the other parties decided on who their candidate should be. Ed Miliband was the first to visit the constituency, going out and about with Andy Sawford in Thrapston on August 9, only three days after Mrs Mensch's resignation. He talked to a group of unemployed youngsters as well as chatting to residents and said: "Two years ago the Conservatives won this seat from Labour. We must persuade those who did not vote Labour last time to put their trust in us again."

UKIP also sent their party leader to the town almost immediately - a clear sign of how seriously we were taking this contest. Nigel

Farage joining the party's candidate, Margot Parker, in Corby on Saturday, August 18, along with the party's local MEPs Roger Helmer and Derek Clark. Mr Farage said: "We intend to put together a serious campaign here. The voters here are angry because they have had the classic A-lister [Louise Mensch] imposed upon them and are now facing an election that many feel is unnecessary."

The other parties did not take this move terribly seriously at the time. A spokesmen for the Tories claimed he had not noticed the Farage visit, though whether that was true or not was not clear. For those of us on the inside of UKIP the fact that Nigel had taken along both regional MEPs was a sign we were serious. Otherwise the three would have made separate visits to try to keep UKIP in the headlines without undue effort.

Another point worth mentioning was that Roger Helmer had been a Conservative MEP until just a few months earlier. He had left after a bruising dispute with the then Conservative Party Chairman Baroness Warsi over exactly the sort of slavish attitude to political correctness that had seen me leave a couple of years earlier. Roger was, we all knew, a talented speaker and had a popular following among the more Eurosceptic Conservative voters of the East Midlands. Deploying him so early in the campaign was a clear sign that Margot was intending to filch Tory voters wherever she could. After all, at this point at least, the attitude of the Tory candidate to the EU was not known for the simple reason that nobody knew who the candidate was going to be.

Meanwhile, it seemed that anybody who was anybody in the Labour Party wanted to get behind Andy Sawford's campaign, shadow chief secretary to the Treasury, Rachel Reeves, joined him at Woodnewton Children's Centre to listen to parents' concerns, on Wednesday, August 29. She said: "The mums that I met today in Corby have been telling me about the difficulties they are facing in order to make ends meet. Increasing food and energy prices are hitting families hard here in Corby and East Northamptonshire."

A day later the Conservatives finally revealed the name of their candidate. Christine Emmett's campaign didn't get off to the best of starts when the first official announcement naming her as the Conservative Party's candidate, late on Friday, August 31, referred to the constituency as Corby and East North Hants. Putting on a brave face, she went out and about in Corby the next day, and said: "Everyone wants a decent house, a good education for their children and a job and those are the issues I'll campaign on."

Next, Andy Sawford launched his Save Our Hospital petition, an issue that was to become one of the main debating points of the campaign. Corby does not have a hospital and its residents rely on nearby Kettering General Hospital (KGH) for their treatment. At the time of the campaign the services offered at the hospital, along with those in Luton, Bedford, Milton Keynes and Northampton were being examined in the Healthier Together review. Many feared the review would lead to a downgrading of services at KGH, a situation which Andy claimed had "left people angry and in disbelief".

Christine Emmett put out a press release on September 27 and in it she quoted Dr Dan Poulter, Under Secretary of State, Department of Health, who said: "Simply put Labour are talking rubbish as there is no chance Kettering Hospital will close. The Healthier Together Group is looking at how services can be improved to benefit the people of Corby and East Northamptonshire. The Conservatives were the only party at the last general election that pledged to increase the NHS budget and in government we are increasing the money going to the frontline - which the people of Corby are seeing the benefit of next week with the opening of a new Urgent Care Centre. As the people of Wales have discovered, where Labour control health budgets they are cutting them."

Meanwhile, the LibDem's Jill Hope said Labour was "frightening people". Talking about Andy Sawford's claims she added: "I think this is totally irresponsible. It is a terrible thing to be doing. People locally are frightened by what's been said."

It was the first week of October by this point and the LibDem campaign was clearly faltering. In the 2010 General Election the LibDems had come third with 14% of the vote. But their once fabled by-election campaign operation was falling to pieces. Jill Hope was

Nigel Farage chats about local issues to UKIP candidate in the Corby By-election on 28 September during one of his visits to the by-election campaign.

failing to get coverage in the media, party workers were thinner on the ground than expected and her local councillors were not seen as often as might have been expected.

The local and national media were still not registering the UKIP effort in Corby. It seems they were obsessed by the Tory vs Labour fight and were not interested in what we were up to. In a way that suited us just fine. By this time our team were reporting a very interesting fact.

Although Margot lived in the rural part of the seat, and our branch members were overwhelmingly from that strong Tory area as well, our team on the streets were finding strong and growing support in the Labour-dominated Corby town. This was something we had noticed to a lesser extent in the Black Country, and I know some

UKIP activists had experienced it elsewhere. But in Corby things seemed different.

Up to this date our experience of UKIP support in traditional Labour areas had been that it seemed to be a protest vote. People were voting for UKIP because we weren't the Labour Party that had so clearly betrayed the interests of the working class, while at the same time we weren't the despised Tory toffs, nor the LibDems who were in coalition with them. Well, in politics you gratefully accept votes where you can find them. If this sort of protest voter helps UKIP to win elections, that is fine by me. However, protest votes are temporary things and rarely last very long.

In Corby our workers knocking on doors were reporting a much more positive tone. This time ex-Labour voters were voting UKIP because they liked UKIP, rather than simply to protest against the modern Labour Party. These things can be difficult to quantify precisely, and affected only some of the area, but there was a definite shift among Labour voters.

On October 12, the BBC reported that the NHS had told them Kettering General Hospital would not be downgraded. But the issue refused to die. On Tuesday, October 16, Labour's shadow health minister Andy Burnham visited the Minor Injuries Unit at Corby and said it wasn't possible to believe Tory promises about the NHS.

UKIP's candidate Margot Parker then weighed into the debate and dismissed Labour's campaign as "a shabby load of nonsense". It was now in our interests to reveal the hypocrisy and dishonesty of the Labour campaign. Disgruntled Labour voters were coming to us, so the more we could expose Labour's failings the more votes we would get.

An issue that was close to the hearts of many rural voters – wind farms – was raised by Christine Emmett when she met residents of the village of Titchmarsh to discuss the issue of onshore wind farms on September 27. Her campaign manager Chris Heaton-Harris MP, an anti-wind farm campaigner, joined her. Christine told residents: "Should a local community choose to accept a wind farm proposal, either because of a financial incentive or any other reason, then it would not be for me to step in their way. However, I would be surprised if the level of compensation developers would give would be enough to tempt many people.

"At the beginning of this month, in my role as a local councillor, I voted against an attempt to force an unwanted wind farm development on a local community. If elected to represent the people of Corby and East Northants I will be sure that the views of my constituents are heard at the highest level and will fight against any unwanted development."

Chris Heaton-Harris added: "Many areas across Northamptonshire have been blighted by wind farm developments."

Sadly for the Conservatives their message still didn't seem to be getting through to the voters. UKIP was also driving hard on the wind farm issue and we were more credible on the subject. Cameron and the Tories had for some years been courting the greenie zealots at the BBC and Guardian with statements slavishly proclaiming global warming to be a catastrophic threat to humanity - even though the planet had not warmed measurably since 2001. And Cameron in particular was fully signed up to the greenie agenda, having promised to make his goverment "the greenest ever". I know that some Tories do not buy into that, and Chris Heaton-Harris is one, but wheeling him out to talk common sense is bound to fail as a tactic when the team captain has so loudly proclaimed the opposite.

UKIP, on the other hand, had never bought into the green-left agenda. And our Energy Spokesman, Roger Helmer MEP, was a powerful voice for common sense. Ironically, Roger used to be a Conservative MEP for the East Midlands with Chris Heaton-Harris as his fellow Tory MEP from 1999 to 2009. It was interesting to watch the public's reactions to the two men speaking about wind farms. Heaton-Harris was heard with polite disbelief due to his party leader's stance. Helmer was welcomed warmly because people knew his party leader supported the policies he put forward.

Obviously it was the credibility of our policies as much as the policies themselves that were winning UKIP support.

On 28 September, UKIP's leader Nigel Farage was back in Corby.

Tellers at a Corby town centre polling station at lunchtime on a rather chilly polling day with Labour on the left and UKIP on the right. Town centre polling stations were manned only by UKIP and Labour, while the rural stations saw UKIP and Tory tellers on duty. Only UKIP was everywhere.

He was paying a flying visit to the party's campaign headquarters in New Post Office Square to praise the party's candidate Margot Parker and her campaign director Lisa Duffy for their hard work. According to a UK Politics poll UKIP were second, just behind Labour in the by-election campaign. Mr Farage said: "This is a fantastic achievement. Each voter is a convert from one of the other parties and they are leaving in droves to join us." This was the first open acknowledgment that UKIP were doing well in Corby. I gather that our street workers had already realised this, but the other parties had been denying it. Now the cat was out of the bag.

With the expected date of the by-election drawing nearer the Tories sent more reinforcements. On Tuesday, October 2, Conservative Party Deputy Chairman Sarah Newton MP joined Christine Emmett for a visit to environmental charity, Phoenix Resource Centre, in Irthlingborough. The next day Parliamentary Under Secretary of State at the Department of Health Anna Soubry MP together with Christine visited Lakelands Hospice in Corby.

Early October was a busy time for UKIP's Margot Parker. On Friday, October 5, she harnessed opposition to wind farms among the constituency's village-dwelling voters when she was joined by Roger Helmer MEP and Derek Clark MEP at Brigstock village hall for a meeting to discuss the issue. This was a tremendous success, with standing room only and an enthusiastic audience.

On Monday, October 8, Margot issued a press release slamming an EU directive that made it illegal for people to sell home-made jam, chutney or marmalade in re-used jam jars, which she called "yet another piece of interfering nonsense". She added: "Can you believe you could actually be flung in jail for six months for selling your home-made preserves in a previously used jam jar?" Then on Thursday, October 11, Paul Nuttall MEP, the party's deputy leader joined Margot at The Cube for a public meeting on open door immigration entitled "Over-crowded Britain?" Once again the meeting was packed out and highly supportive.

These public meetings have gone out of fashion with the clever young things who run campaigns for LibLabCon, but they have a lot to offer if handled correctly. A public meeting can get you in touch with the voters in a way that focus groups cannot. In the context of a by-election, it can help to build momentum as people come along and realise that they are not alone in supporting UKIP, but part of a growing movement. That encourages them to actually go and vote for UKIP, not just sit at home moaning at the TV every time David Cameron comes on the screen.

On Tuesday, October 23, the day the date of the by-election was officially announced as Thursday, November 15, the Conservatives received more bad news when the results of a poll commissioned by Tory grandee and former deputy party chairman Lord Ashcroft were released. They showed that Labour had established a 22 per cent lead over the Tories because voters wanted to punish the Government.

However, the survey of 1,503 voters in the constituency suggested the Tories might be able to win back voters in the constituency by the time of the next General Election in 2015 as Labour was not trusted to run the economy.

A hustings event was held in the Great Hall at Oundle School on Sunday, November 4, chaired by the political correspondent for Channel 4 News, Michael Crick and featuring Christine Emmett, Andy Sawford, Jill Hope and Margot Parker. This was a clear sign that Channel 4, at least, was taking UKIP seriously as a contender even if the other parties were not.

Travelling the constituency it was easy to see it dividing on town versus country lines. 'Support Labour' posters adorned streets in Corby, along with a good smattering of UKIP posters. While fields in the more rural areas, particularly near Oundle, had huge Conservative posters in them, but again there were UKIP posters. It was quite obvious that UKIP and only UKIP were getting support from both halves of the constituency. This was a fact that would be confirmed over the coming months and would feed into UKIP strategy for the County elections of 2013 and Euro elections of 2014.

It was in the wake of the hustings that members of Andy Sawford's party told a reporter of their delight at UKIP's Margot Parker's strong showing, which (they said) was bound to affect the Conservative vote. Little did they know how much it would affect their vote too.

The final few days of electioneering started with a bit of razzmatazz as Mr Mozzarella, of the Don't Cook Party, visited the area, arriving in Coronation Park in Corby by jet-propelled backpack. He then went into the town centre to spread his message that people should be freed from the kitchen and cooking, which is "choppy, choppy, messy, messy". Accompanied by cheerleaders and a face painter, he attracted a lot of attention. Bringing her own bit of showbusiness to the campaign, Margot Parker organised an event with writer, broadcaster and UKIP supporter Mike Read at The Cube, on Monday, November 12. Margot continued to tell people that every vote cast for UKIP is a vote from one of the other parties. She said she was hoping to get votes from Conservatives who were disenchanted with the coalition and from disaffected voters who feel they have been betrayed by Labour policies which created a mountain of debt and free-for-all immigration. A reporter wrote this up and called the claim to get votes off Labour as being "perhaps a little surprising". Yet another sign of how slow those innured to the LibLabCon world were to see what was happening.

Margot went on to say that people were willing to give her their vote because: "UKIP is seen as telling the truth, valuing the voter who gives their vote but above all listening to the people; never shying away from the thorny issues of immigration, job losses and availability and, above all, avoiding the spin which so undervalues the intelligence of our constituents." On Wednesday, November 14, Margot returned to the subject and added: "UKIP will never try to out-guess the voters and the outcome tomorrow is awaited with quiet confidence in the voters of Corby and East Northants to select the candidate that means what she says."

Election Day in Corby was cold and murky, not ideal weather for persuading people to go to the polling stations. A number of Labour MPs, including Liam Byrne, Toby Perkins, Caroline Flint and Chuka Umunna, were out doing last minute door knocking for Andy Sawford. Chuka Umunna sent a cheeky tweet saying he had been out to Cameron Court in Corby and the first house had a Labour poster in the window.

UKIP made their presence felt by towing a huge UKIP sign round the constituency and Margot Parker said she got a good reaction with people giving her the thumbs up and calling out to tell her they had voted for her. She was also interviewed by Dutch TV, The Daily Express and PA.

More tellingly, I think, was the sheer number of UKIP activists on the ground. There were UKIP tellers at all the bigger polling stations, right across the constituency. Labour did not bother in the villages, Conservatives did not bother in the town. UKIP did. That showed the purple and yellow flag clearly enough, but UKIP also had teams out banging on doors and encouraging people to vote. This was a big effort by our party and the result showed that UKIP was able to mobilise supporters to travel and campaign in areas outside their own - not a traditional strength of UKIP.

As election day drew to a close, Question Time was held in Kingswood School, Corby. On the panel were justice secretary Chris Grayling, Labour's deputy leader and shadow culture secretary Harriet Harman, Tessa Munt of the Lib Dems, UKIP leader Nigel Farage and the chief executive of M&C Saatchi, Moray MacLennan. Chris Grayling praised Christine Emmett for her campaign but seemed to concede defeat, explaining that mid-term elections are always difficult for the party in power.

Nigel Farage, who is always value for money, predicted that Labour would win comfortably, adding that the Lib Dems' candidate Jill Hope had no hope and said there was nothing to choose between the three main parties. A member of the audience seemed to echo this sentiment when he said that UKIP had been "a breath of fresh air".

The count at Lodge Park Sports Centre in Corby attracted national media interest, with 10 news organisations present. To those who could see into the counting hall it was obvious by lunch time who the winner was, as the boxes with Andy Sawford's name on stacked up. There was some last minute drama as the Lib Dems asked for two recounts, but in the end they had a poor showing and Jill Hope lost her deposit.

The returning officer, Paul Goult, finally announced the results at about 3pm. The turnout was 44.78 per cent, with 35,775 votes cast. Andy Sawford got 17,267 votes and his Conservative rival, Christine Emmett, 9,476. UKIP came third with 5,108 votes. This gave them 14 per cent of the vote and was the party's best showing in a by-election. Speaking afterwards, UKIP's Margot Parker also warned Andy she would be "keeping an eye on him and watching him to make sure he keeps his promises".

Coming third with 14% was a significant improvement on recent by-election results that had seen UKIP get a string of 4th and 5th positions. As it transpired things were only going to get better.

Even while the Corby dust was settling, things were hotting up in Croydon North, in south London. The by-election there was held two weeks after Corby, on 29 November 2012, the same day as two other by-elections: Rotherham and Middlesborogh. The results of the votes on 29 November would prove to be a spectacular triple whammy of success for UKIP.

The by-election in Croydon North was an unusual one from the start. With so many contests going on elsewhere, neither the media nor national political figures had much time for this area of south London. Just for once a parliamentary by-election was largely left to local people and local campaigners to slog it out on local issues. It was a unique event, as we shall see.

This was a staunchly Labour constituency, and as such UKIP was not expected to do well. At the 2010 General Election, Labour had come top with 56% of the vote, the Conservatives second with 24% and UKIP fifth with 1.7%. The pundits were predicting something similar in the by-election, but on the bounce after our success in Corby, we in UKIP were not so sure. We now knew that we were taking votes from Labour in some numbers, and that the voters switching to us were increasingly doing so for positive reasons, not just as a protest vote.

The by-election was caused by the death of highly respected MP for Croydon North, Malcolm Wicks, on 20 September 2012. This came as a shock to most as although he had been suffering from cancer for some time this fact was not widely known. He had represented Croydon North since 1992 and during the Labour governments of Tony Blair and Gordon Brown held a number of ministerial posts, including those of energy, pensions and science. Out of respect to Mr Wicks, campaigning did not get going until after the funeral.

In 2010 Croydon North became a Conservative-free zone for the

*A polling station in Croydon North early on the day of the
2012 By-election that saw UKIP support surge.*

first time in its history. Nor were other parties represented as neither
the Liberal Democrats nor any of the other smaller parties - Greens,
Christian Peoples Alliance, UKIP and Communists among them -
managed to win a single council ward. However, the political
landscape was not as monochrome as the mass of Labour councillors
might suggest. In Upper Norwood the Conservatives were not all that
far behind Labour and the Liberal Democrats had racked up sizeable
votes in most areas. Where they stood the Greens had also counted
their votes by the hundred, and although UKIP stood only two

candidates they did not disgrace themselves. There was also a new kid on the block in the form of the Respect Party. This party got only 275 votes in the 2010 General Election, but was quietly organising behind the scenes.

Labour chose their candidate on the afternoon of Saturday 5 November. It turned out to be Steve Reed. First of the non-Labour candidates to be announced was the Liberal Democrat Marisha Ray. Her candidacy was announced on 17 October after an evening meeting of the Croydon North Liberal Democrat Party.

Next to enter the fray was the UKIP candidate Winston McKenzie, who was announced on 18 October. McKenzie was born in Jamaica, but moved to Britain at a young age and became Middleweight, All England Amateur Boxing Champion in 1975. He then retired from boxing and turned to running a pub in Thornton Heath, though by the time of the by-election he was working as a youth worker. After a short spell in the Conservative Party, McKenzie joined the United Kingdom Independence Party (UKIP) in 2009. The following year he was the UKIP candidate for Tottenham in the General Election and in 2012 stood to be London Assembly Member for Croydon and Sutton.

With a colourful past behind him, McKenzie was widely expected to bring some surprises and humour to the campaign. He did not disappoint as a journalist remembered seeing McKenzie performing a rap song in Croydon while wearing a fetching pale pink suit and broad-brimmed black fedora. The performance was still on Youtube and quickly became a short-lived cult hit in Croydon.

On 19 October it was the turn of the Conservatives to announce their candidate. Andy Stranack was born in Croydon and worked for Croydon Jubilee Church as a Community Development Worker. It was ironic that he worked with Malcolm Wicks on some projects.

Then came news from an unexpected quarter. David Icke, campaigner for "New Age Spiritiualism" put out a public appeal for anyone who lived in Croydon North and who shared his views to get in touch. Speculation mounted that there would be a candidate from the New Age movement.

The Respect Party, as long expected, announced they would be standing on 23 October. They chose Lee Jasper, who had gained fame in London as Mayor Ken Livingstone's Director for Policing and Equalities from 2004 to 2008. He had been responsible for the development and delivery of anti discriminatory policies aimed at ensuring equality in employment practices and service delivery. He was also directly responsible for advising the Mayor on policing issues. Announcing Lee Jasper's candidacy, the Respect MP George Galloway said "If I could have composed the perfect candidate to fight this seat then it would be Lee Jasper." Minutes later Jasper tweeted: "I am delighted to have been selected now let's roll up our sleeves & do the work, No more talk time for action."

The British National Party (BNP) put forward as their candidate Richard Edmonds, the party's Deputy Chairman. The Christian Peoples Alliance announced that Stephen Hammond would be their candidate. The Communist Party put up Ben Stevenson. Simon Lane stood for the Nine Eleven Was An Inside Job Party. Robin Smith stood for the Young People's Party. Meanwhile, the Greens announced that their candidate would be Sasha Khan, described as a "community campaigner". For the first time in four years the Official Monster Raving Loony Party stood in a Parliamentary By-election in the shape of John Cartwright, a local Croydon man.

In a Parliamentary election, be it a General Election or a By-election, every candidate is given the opportunity to have one leaflet delivered free of charge by the Royal Mail to every elector in the constituency. These leaflets have to conform to a set of rules concerning their size, layout and content. They cannot, for instance, ask for money or seek to recruit new party members. Generally, however, they can say pretty much whatever the candidate wants.

A great deal of agonised debate goes on among candidates and their campaign teams as to what this free delivery should consist of. The traditional option is for the free delivery to consist of the "Election Address", a sort of mini-manifesto highlighting the key policies of the candidate that is usually printed on a sheet of A4 paper, folded into three so that it goes through letterboxes easily. Since the early 1990s, however, the free deliveries have become more varied. Some candidates have chosen to send out a letter, others to have a leaflet delivered that doubles as a window poster and some - perhaps short on money - have gone for small A5 flyers. Although delivery is free, the candidate still has to pay for the leaflet itself, which explains why bigger parties go for glossy, full colour leaflets and others for black and white efforts on cheap paper.

For a smaller party short of the sorts of funds the Tories and Labour can deploy, the free delivery is a blessing. UKIP always tries to ensure that the free delivery presents their policies and candidate in as fair and balanced fashion as possible, while emphasising those points most likely to garner votes in the area in question.

In addition to the free delivery leaflet, candidates can deliver as many pieces of paper as they wish. These leaflets are not constrained by the same rules as the free delivery, so they very often ask for money, seek to recruit members or come in big A3 format, or as little A6 business cards. They can be a highly varied mix.

Whatever tactics a candidate chooses to pursue, there are strict rules on how much money can be spent and what it can be spent on. While the limits in a by-election are fairly generous, being in the tens of thousands of pounds, no candidate is allowed to buy a voter food or drink, and all candidates have to be aware that the usual rules on libel and slander apply when they are talking about a rival candidate.

Labour and the Conservatives opted for conventional tactics: delivering leaflets with glossy colour photos of their candidates and an assortment of fairly bland policy promises.

Ken Livingstone, Labour's former Mayor of London, came to Croydon on 12 November to campaign for Steve Reed. There had earlier been some speculation that Livingstone may have privately been backing his former deputy Lee Jasper, but Livingstone made his views clear. "I am backing Steve Reed because he is fighting for the Living Wage, which I pioneered as Mayor of London and which he has introduced as leader of Lambeth Council. He will also lead the fight against the blight of youth unemployment and bring jobs and regeneration to Croydon North."

On 19 November Croydon was diverted by the arrival in town of Boris Johnson, Conservative Mayor of London, who came to campaign with Andy Stranack around local shops. Perhaps predictably, far more people recognised Boris than Andy, but the mayor did a sterling job of introducing the Tory candidate to anyone he could find, pouncing on unsuspecting passersby to deliver a merry quip before bounding off to find a new recipient for his wit. For those who have seen Boris in action before, it was a classic performance, but it may have left the average Thornton Heath shopper somewhat bemused.

On 20 November the much anticipated public hustings took place, chaired by the editor of the Croydon Advertiser. The meeting room at Gonville Academy was packed. Reed and Stranack were by this date clearly seen as the front runners, but all candidates were allowed an equal share of time. Reed and Stranack led on the issues of unemployment, the economy and representing the people of Croydon. Jasper responded vigorously. "We're 'real' Labour, you're 'fake' Labour" he claimed at one point. At one point the meeting threatened to degenerate into a slanging match between Reed and Jasper, with the other candidates looking on from the sidelines, but skilful chairmanship moved things along. The Green Party's Sasha Khan spoke at length about the proposed industrial incinerator and about education. Marisha Ray for the LibDems also spoke about education and had a good grasp of her party's policies on a range of issues.

UKIP's Winston McKenzie, as might be expected, spoke most about the European Union. He was generally thought to have performed well, but all media eyes were on the Tory and Labour.

But his campaign suffered a blow the next day. Sensing a surge in their vote in Rotherham - where a by-election was to be held the same day - UKIP told all its supporters to abandon Croydon and go north instead. Of course many activists in London did not want to make the long journey and continued to slog away in Croydon. Nevertheless the fact that our national organisation felt able to make this call showed that the drive to professionalise the party was really getting a grip. We were targeting seriously and our members were responding. Inevitably, the move dealt a blow to MacKenzie, but by all accounts he took it in good part and understood the reasons.

Polling stations opened on Thursday 29 November at 7am. At five minutes to 7 Tory candidate Andy Stranack tweeted "Polls for the #Croydon North by-election open in 5 mins. Today won't change the Government, vote for someone like you." Steve Reed was only seconds behind him, choosing Facebook rather than Twitter to post his early morning message. "The polls are open in Croydon North and voting has begun. Thanks everyone for all your help and support. Let's use today to send a message to Downing Street that people are hurting because this Government's not working, and let's give people back the hope of a better future."

Respect were touring the constituency in an open topped bus festooned with balloons and posters. Riding on top, well muffled against the cold were activists. Fighting the chilly wind they did a good job of looking enthusiastic while one of them harangued the crowds to go out and vote for Lee Jasper.

UKIP also opted for a loud speaker system, though they had a van towing a small trailer on which was rigged up a big purple and yellow poster proclaiming "Vote UKIP". Despite such noisy efforts, the turn out at Polling Stations remained low throughout the day. By the time polling stations closed at 10pm a total of 24,562 people had voted, a turnout of 26.53%. It was low, but it could have been worse.

As is traditional in Britain, the counting of votes took place immediately after polling stations closed on the Thursday evening. This makes for a long day, but it has several advantages. First the result is known immediately. Second the opportunities for anyone to tamper with the ballot boxes is kept to a minimum.

The first stage in the count is to verify the votes. This means that the votes in each individual ballot box are counted to see if they tally with the number of people recorded as going to vote at that polling station. This stops any dishonest person from stuffing a few hundred extra votes for their preferred candidate into the ballot box. Each ballot paper has what is known as the "mark" on it. This is a set of perforations set out in a pattern that changes for each election and is designed to stop papers from one election being fraudulently used in the next. Once these formalities are over, and all the candidates and agents are happy there has been no dishonesty, the count proper begins.

Ballot papers are first sorted into piles for each candidate. Each pile is then passed to a second counter who checks that all the votes are for the same candidate. A third counter then counts the pile of votes into bundles of fifty papers, again checking they are all for the same candidate. A fourth counter then checks that each bundle contains fifty votes for the same candidate. Throughout this entire process the counters are watched by volunteers appointed by the candidates. Everything is done to ensure that no cheating takes place. Even so, there are incidents when what are usually termed "mistakes" are made, though some candidates or their agents have made allegations of cheating.

Once the votes are bundled into fifties, checked and verified, they are put into baskets with each candidate having a different basket. In most elections it is clear early on which candidate is ahead. Once all the votes have been bundled and transferred to baskets they are actually counted. The bundles are counted in multiples of fifty, and spares counted individually.

The Returning Officer, who is in charge of the whole process, then summons the candidates or their agents to consult them on disputed papers. These are ballot papers where the intention of the voter was not clear to the counters. The consultation with the candidates and agents is a courtesy as the final decision lies with the Returning Officer. Taken one at a time, each disputed ballot paper is inspected by all present, then the Returning Officer decides if it should be counted for one or other of the candidates or if it should be declared to be "spoilt" and set aside.

Once the disputed papers are dealt with the Returning Officer does a final count of all votes and checks with his or her deputy that the final count is agreed. The agents or candidates are then summoned again and told the result. The candidates then have the opportunity to ask for a recount. This usually occurs if the candidate lying second is only 2% or 3% behind the winner. The bundles are then recounted and the spares added up again. It is usual for a "bundle check" to take place. This means that each bundle is flipped through to ensure all the votes are for the same person and that the bundle is in the correct basket. After the recount a second recount may be requested if the result is very close. After this the final result is then declared.

There were no such problems at Croydon North. Labour's Steve Reed was so far out in front that Conservative Andy Stranack accepted the result immediately. The final results were as follows.

Steve Reed (Lab) 15,898 (64.71% of the vote, up 8.69%)
Andy Stranack (C) 4,137 (16.84% of the vote, down 7.28%)
Winston McKenzie (UKIP) 1,400 (5.70% of the vote, up 3.97%)
Marisha Ray (LD) 860 (3.50% of the vote, down 10.48%)
Shasha Islam Khan (Green) 855 (3.48% of the vote, up 1.51%)
Lee Jasper (Respect) 707 (2.88% of the vote, up 2.35%)
Stephen Hammond (CPA) 192 (0.78% of the vote)
Richard Edmonds (NF) 161 (0.66% of the vote)
Ben Stevenson (Comm) 119 (0.48% of the vote, up 0.17%)
John Cartwright (Loony) 110 (0.45% of the vote)
Simon Lane (Nine eleven) 66 (0.27% of the vote)
Robin Smith (Young) 63 (0.26% of the vote)
Labour majority 11,761 (47.87% of the vote)

It was a convincing win for Labour and a blow for the Conservatives. The Liberal Democrats had crashed very badly. They had gone from 14% of the vote in 2010 to just 3.5%. This terrible result was even worse than might have been expected from the national opinion polls, which themselves had recently been making depressing reading for LibDem HQ. The result for Respect was also crushing. Throughout the campaign they had been portraying themselves as the left wing alternative to Labour and promising to hoover up large numbers of votes from Labour voters disgruntled with Ed Milliband's leadership. The media had, on the whole, taken these claims at face value and given Respect a lot of coverage. The final tally of 2.88% of votes was a slap in the face to Respect and their claims. Like the LibDems Respect lost their deposit, always considered something of a humiliation in British politics.

By contrast, UKIP did very well. We got 5.7%, up 4% on 2010 and leapfrogged up to third place.

Running alongside the Croydon North vote were two other by-elections: in Rotherham and in Middlesbrough.

The sudden death of Sir Stuart Bell, MP for Middlesbrough, came as a real shock to all who knew him. The by-election that followed started off with all the hallmarks of being one of the dullest on record. Labour had a huge majority in Middlesbrough and there were no local issues that looked like they might change that. The town was solid Labour Party territory, and had been for generations. Not only that but with two other by-elections due to take place on the same day - in Croydon North and Rotherham - it seemed that the media and the politicians would be spread thinly and few would have time to spare for safe Labour Middlesbrough.

The make up of the borough reflects Labour's traditional dominance in the area. After the local elections of 2011 Labour had 30 councillors, the Conservatives 4 and the LibDems 1, with 13 Independents. The councillors in the Middlesbrough constituency are almost solidly Labour, with just one Conservative flying the blue flag.

The General Election results for the constituency confirm Labour's control. In 2010 Sir Stuart Bell got over 15,000 votes with the Conservatives and Liberal Democrats on 6,000 apiece. In 2005 Bell had 18,000 votes, with second place Liberal Democrats on 6,000. Even at the height of Conservative fortunes in 1983, Bell got 21,000 votes to the Tory's 11,000. Middlesbrough has never been anything other than Labour.

First to announce a candidate were the Liberal Democrats who put forward George Selmer. Selmer had been born and educated in the town, but had since moved away. On being selected he issued a statement to the press with regard to this.

The Labour candidate was local lawyer Andy McDonald, who came out to say to the waiting press "I am overwhelmed and humbled by the support I have received. It has been absolutely magnificent. I am a Boro lad and this is one of the proudest moments of my life.

There is a real jobs crisis on Teesside. Too many of our young people are being left without a future and families are really struggling with the cost of living. The fight for jobs will be a priority for me. This Tory-led government is completely out of touch with the lives of people here in Middlesbrough. Their economic policies are causing real pain. Over the next few weeks I will be campaigning in every part of the town, listening to local people and also talking with them about how I can bring real change to Middlesbrough. The campaign starts now. I can't wait to get started."

The Conservatives chose their candidate in the form of Ben Houchen, who worked in the constituency. In his opening statement, Houchen said: "It was a privilege to be selected as the Conservative candidate for Middlesbrough. Being born and bred here I really relish the opportunity to campaign for the community that has given me so much during my life. It's a dream come true to be selected as the candidate for my home town."

Of the smaller parties, the most high profile was obviously UKIP. We put forward Richard Elvin who had stood in the 2010 General Election in nearby Houghton and was our regional Chairman for North East England. He declared that "It is time for radical new policies which are only offered by UKIP."

Richard Elvin began by promoting Alistair Baxter, the UKIP PCC candidate. It was not until after the 15 November that his Facebook page switched to campaigning for himself. By that date the polls were showing a big increase in support for UKIP nationally and we had the Corby result to buoy us along, though it was unclear if that would translate into support in Middlesbrough. The UKIP campaign really got under way on 17 November when an empty shop near the town centre was rented for two weeks to serve as campaign HQ. That afternoon Elvin and a team of helpers were out in the shopping centre handing out UKIP leaflets to the shoppers.

On 23 November news broke that would radically change the campaign for UKIP. In Rotherham, where another by-election was being fought, the Labour council had removed children from an otherwise blameless foster family due to the fact that they voted

UKIP. The news provoked a storm of anti-Labour news stories and in Rotherham stoked the UKIP vote. The national UKIP leadership ordered all effort in Middlesbrough to cease and instructed all their workers to converge on Rotherham. Within hours almost the only UKIP activist still in the town was candidate Richard Elvin.

He did not complain, but gamely bashed on with his campaigning. A trailer able to display posters was acquired, plastered with Elvin posters and sent out to drive about. It was an effective method of reminding voters that UKIP and Elvin existed and prominently displayed the three key messages of "End open-door immigration"; "Stop taxing workers on the minimum wage"; and "Rebuild our world-beating manufacturing industries", but there was no way to hide the fact that it was less effective than having boots on the ground.

The evening of 26 November saw a hustings meeting take place in St Barnabas Church, Linthorpe, organised by Friends of the Earth. It got off to a bumpy start. The BNP candidate had not been invited, Chair of the meeting, Simon Bowens, explained "The BNP were not invited because of Friends of the Earth's strict policy of not engaging with them because of their views on race and immigration, which are contrary to ours." Mr Foreman turned up anyway and organised a noisy protest against what he claimed was an attack on freedom of speech. A policeman who was present spoke to Foreman who left peacefully having made his point. Foreman was, however, interviewed by the BBC and managed to make a few points.

As the count progressed, news came in that the UKIP vote was surging in Croydon North and Rotherham. As the votes for UKIP piled up, Elvin and his supporters became increasingly noisy and jubilant. There was no chance he could win, but he was doing very well and as his votes began to outstrip those of the Conservatives and the LibDems, his helpers stood in a line to wave placards in the air.

The final result was declared at just past 1am. The final figures were:

Andy McDonald (Labour)	10,201
Richard Elvin (UKIP)	1,990
George Selmer (Liberal Democrat)	1,672

Ben Houchen (Conservative)	1,063
Imdad Hussain (Peace)	1,060
Peter Foreman (BNP)	328
John Malcolm (TUSC)	277
Mark Heslehurst (Independent)	275
Labour majority:	8,211

Each of the candidates then made a short speech. As is traditional each began by thanking the Returning Officer and his staff for their efficient work, the Police for keeping order and their own party workers for all their help.

UKIP's Richard Elvin declared "There can be no doubt that UKIP is on the up. UKIP is now the only political party which we can truly say can take the fight to Labour in the North East."

The analysts then began poring over the figures. They showed that Labour's share of the vote had gone up by 14%, the Conservatives down by 10% and the LibDems down by 12.5%. The BNP vote had collapsed by two thirds. But the big story of the night was the increase in the UKIP vote. Their share had gone from just over 1% to 11%. Combined with equally impressive results in the other two by-elections it confirmed a big surge in UKIP support. Given that the final week had seen virtually no UKIP activity in Middlesbrough the vote there was particularly impressive. There was even talk of UKIP replacing the LibDems as the third party in English politics.

Coming second in Middlesbrough was a tremendous result for Richard Elvin and UKIP. Even better was the result in Rotherham. The campaign there was proceeding in orderly fashion, but spectacularly exploded a week before polling day when as mentioned previously a Rotherham couple contacted the Daily Telegraph with an astonishing story. They had been fostering children for seven years, when a pair of children were suddenly and unceremoniously removed from them by Labour-run Rotherham's social services on the grounds that they voted UKIP.

The wife told the Daily Telegraph: "I was dumbfounded. Then my question to both of them was, 'What has UKIP got to do with having the children removed?' Then one of them said, 'Well, UKIP have got racist policies.' The implication was that we were racist. [The social worker] said UKIP does not like European people and wants them all out of the country to be returned to their own countries." The paper reported that the woman denied she was racist but the children were taken away by the end of the week. She said the social worker told her: "We would not have placed these children with you had we known you were members of UKIP because it wouldn't have been the right cultural match." The couple said they had been "stigmatised and slandered".

There were several disturbing features about this. First, that the social services felt justified in removing foster children from care because of the political views of the foster parents. Second, that the policies of UKIP are nothing like those stated by the social worker - indicating that she had acted out of raw prejudice and had not researched UKIP's policies. Third, and to me the most disturbing of all, was the fact that when Rotherham Borough Council's Strategic Director of Children and Young People's Services, Joyce Thacker was challenged about this, she immediately defended the action. She said "If the party mantra is, for example, ending the active promotion of multiculturalism I have to think about that."

Her attitude played right into what so many of us in UKIP believe is wrong about Britain today. She has her own lefty views about supporting and actively promoting multiculturalism. If you don't agree with her political agenda, you are to be stripped of your role as foster parents. This dictatorial attitude shows why the left-wing establishment need to be taken down a peg or two.

UKIP leader Nigel Farage condemned the decision and said the council had many questions to answer. He told the BBC he felt: "Very upset and very angry... this couple involved who have been fostering for many years and are very decent people. This was an awful shock to them, not to mention the upset for the children themselves. Politically, I am not surprised at all. This is typical of the bigotry you get from the Labour party and Labour controlled councils. We have nothing against people from Poland or elsewhere in the world... we are not against immigration. We believe in controlled immigration."

He added in a statement: "They [the council] have to look at themselves in the mirror and ask who it is that is prejudiced? A normal couple who have fostered for seven years, or themselves who are blinded by political bias? Publicly they must make absolutely clear the decision-making process in this case, who was responsible for this decision and why."

The story exploded over the streets of Rotherham. Within days Labour realised how much damage was being done to them. A Labour spokesman said "Membership of UKIP should not block parents from adopting children. There needs to be an urgent investigation by Rotherham Borough Council into this decision." The local Labour council, however, remained unrepentant.

Our central party, quite rightly, decided to throw everything at Rotherham. Members from across the country were urged to go to Rotherham to deliver leaflets or bang on doors. Our candidate, Jane Collins, proved more than equal to the task. Suddenly thrust into the national media spotlight, she performed confidently and smoothly without compromising any of her integrity. She was already a leading activist in the Yorkshire area, having stood for us in the Barnsley West by-election of March 2011. She would go on to be top Euro candidate for UKIP in the Yorkshire and the Humber region in 2014.

When the votes were finally counted the result was awesome. Labour came top with 46.5% of the vote, UKIP came second with an amazing 21.7%. The Conservatives were fifth with 5.4% (narrowly saving their deposit), while the LibDems cam seventh with a deeply embarrassing 2.7%, down 14% on the general election.

This astonishing run of by-elections was not yet over. Everyone in politics knew that Chris Huhne, MP for Eastleigh, was facing criminal charges and that, if found guilty, he would be forced to resign his seat and trigger another by-election. In the event, Huhne decided to plead guilty on 5 February 2013 and resign his seat. The election was called for 28 February. This was a very short campaign, and everyone thought the LibDems had made this decision to capitalise on their local strength and deny other parties the chance to mobilise their support.

The Eastleigh by-election was one of the most important events in the history of UKIP. With hindsight it was a campaign that carried on the good work of the ground breaking efforts in Rotherham and Corby. Those campaigns had shown the beginnings of a UKIP surge that would carry on to great effect in Eastleigh. It did not start off appearing that way. In fact it was expected to be a walk over for the Conservative party following the disgrace of sitting Lib Dem MP Chris Huhne.

I was certanly not taking much notice of it until an unexpected phone call one Sunday evening while I was drinking my customary couple of pints of real ale in local free house The Beacon Hotel. Now, the beer brewed at the Beacon Hotel is famously strong and I was just starting my second pint of the dark, delicious but deadly Ruby Mild when a phone call came through on my mobile from an undisclosed number. Thinking nothing of it I picked up and casually said hello to find the caller was Nigel Farage.

Nigel made it clear that he was down in Eastleigh and felt there was something in the air and that we had a chance of a pretty incredible votes haul. He then he told me he wanted me down there at the earliest possible opportunity. No sooner had I got off the phone than I contacted Jill Seymour, who had worked very closely with me during the police and crime commissioner campaign. We travelled down together the next day.

Arriving quite late we had no time to do any campaigning and we just booked into our rooms at the Travel Inn. As I was settling in I was delighted to get a phone call from Nigel inviting me to join him for a beer next door at the Weatherspoons pub. We had a couple of pints and a good chat about our mutual love of cricket. As we left, Nigel stopped outside for a cigarette and I stood talking to him with further cricketing anecdotes being exchanged. We had noticed a few sideways looks coming our way from a group of teenage lads in the bar and it was no surprise when they left the pub and approached us. They started by asking "Are you that Farage bloke". When he confirmed his identity, the youths took a hostile line asking him what he was doing in their town and telling him he stood no chance of getting any support. After initially being on my guard to be ready to physically protect Nigel, by the end of the conversation the personal charm, warmth and charisma of the UKIP leader had won the young men over to the point where they were asking for autographs. It was a masterful display of how to deal with the public and how to defuse hostility with straight talking and honesty.

The next day we went out on the campaign trail in Eastleigh. We began with a walk around the town centre starting out at the UKIP shop. UKIP shops have become a standard part of any by-election campaign with a premises on the high street available for the public and media to approach as well as for planning operations. The walkabout through Eastleigh was almost presidential in style with Nigel and Diane James leading a crowd of UKIP activists and assorted media through the high street with shoppers and innocent bystanders almost crushed in the stampede. After the initial excitement had calmed down we broke into smaller groups to go out onto the doorsteps canvassing. In true UKIP style we managed to cram a record number of people into a small car driven by Kirsten Farage. When we arrived at our destination and opened the car doors activists, posters and placards exploded out of the car as they had been so tightly packed in. On knocking on doors I found a fascinating response.

The doorsteps in Eastleigh showed a tremendous amount of disillusionment with the big political parties. The national leadership of those parties were despised by the majority of the people I spoke with. There was a feeling little short of betrayal and a desire to exact revenge by supporting the insurgents of UKIP. Unfortunately for us there was another factor on the doorsteps. Many of the people I spoke to had a very high regard for their local Lib Dem Councillors. These councillors had taken on the role of community workers and had transcended politics. Everybody knew who their local councillor was and they all trusted them to look after the day to day issues that concerned them. This had gained the Lib Dems a high degree of loyalty, it was almost as if their local politicians had erased the stain of the untrustworthiness of their senior people. This was all the more

*The author campaigning with Nigel Farage on the streets of
Eastleigh during the by-election of 2013.*

remarkable in a by-election caused by a criminal conviction to a
sitting Lib Dem MP for lying in court.

After that first visit to Eastleigh I wrote a letter to the press and
circulated it to local UKIP members to urge them to follow me down
to Eastleigh.

*It seemed only right to me that as a UKIP activist I should
lend a day to the campaign in Eastleigh.*

*I managed to book a day off work and teamed up with a
friend to car share. All that remained now was to find out where
Eastleigh actually was! Fortunately the Sat Nav was a lot more
specific than my original set of directions given to Jill Seymour
who was driving us there. "It's somewhere down south" I had*

declared with confidence. Anyway nearly 3 hours after setting out we arrived in the latest political battleground in UKIP's ongoing war to gate crash the establishment parties' fun and get seats at Westminster.

It didn't take us long to find the UKIP campaign head quarters. A shop on the high street had been garishly decorated in UKIP Banners and there was quite a crowd of activists gathering. UKIPers from all round the country had gathered to support the excellent candidate Diane Jones and party leader Nigel Farage.

Media of all sorts were descending on the scene from every direction. Photographers taking a scatter gun approach and recording every movement of the activists before closing in on Nigel Farage as their prime target.

After satisfying the immediate demands of the press Nigel led the assembled UKIP team on a walkabout around the town, struggling to keep up with the hectic pace we trailed in his wake, chatting to people as we went. Members of the public ran the risk of being trampled under foot in the charge of activists and media but none of them were resentful or unhappy. It was more a case of looking at the energy of the UKIP team with a smile and an air of being genuinely impressed

One elderly gentleman stopped me and told me that he had immigrated to this country in the 1950s because he loved our way of life. He very forcefully made the point that UKIP were the only party fighting to preserve the Britain he loved. He would not let me go until I had promised we would all work hard to save our country

After the invigorating charge around the town we split into a separate group to go canvassing on the door steps. The journey to the outlying area in a car full of UKIPers being driven by somebody with no idea where they should be going is one I will always remember. When we finally spilled out of the car, digging people out from under several tonnes of leaflets, we wasted no time getting to work.

The area we went in to was classic working class territory and I was prepared for the kind of debate I get on many of the doorsteps in my home area of Dudley where Labour are very deeply entrenched. I was, however very surprised. I hardly found any Labour voters but I found two main groups. The first was something that pleased me and the second was something I had never encountered before. The first group were people who had enthusiastically converted to UKIP. The other group were Lib Dems...before visiting Eastleigh I don't think I had ever met a Lib Dem and here were loads of them!

The reason for this bizarre finding of a group of people less populous than unicorns in my home town was a simple one. The Lib Dems hold the council in Eastleigh and by all accounts work very hard. At a time when almost everyone was disenchanted with national politics the Lib Dems had taken the saying "All politics is local" to new extremes.

My abiding memories of the campaign in Eastleigh will be the energy of the UKIP team, the disenchantment of the public with the old parties, that crazy journey out to go canvassing but most of all the old gentleman asking us to keep fighting to save our country.

Regardless of the result in Eastleigh it's quite obvious we have momentum and energy as a party. What we must do is keep on building and working hard. I made that old man a promise and I don't believe that our party will let him down.

As it turned out, my first visit to Eastleigh came about half way through the campaign. I was to go back, but the UKIP by-election team were working hard throughout. Nigel had been right to tell me that he could smell something in the air. The campaign was exhilarating.

The town of Eastleigh, on the River Itchen in Hampshire, only really became important in the late 1830s with the coming of the railways, when a station was built there on the Winchester to Southampton line. The town's other claims to fame include being the birthplace of Benny Hill. He spent some time working as a milkman for Hanns Dairies, a job which gave him the inspiration for his famous song "Ernie, The Fastest Milkman in The West".

Politically, the borough council is made up of 44 councillors. After the latest elections in 2012 the Lib Dems had 40 councillors and the Conservatives the remaining four; the Lib Dems having gained two seats from the Independent Party of Eastleigh Councillors.

The Lib Dems have held the seat in five parliamentary elections but it is not regarded as a safe seat, with Mr Huhne only winning the 2005 election by 568 votes, and owing much of his success in the 2010 General Election to tactical voting by Labour voters who preferred him to the Tory candidate. With the Labour Party buoyed by its success in the Corby and East Northamptonshire by-election mounting a strong campaign this time around that was unlikely to happen again. The Conservatives also knew that it would only take a swing of 3.5 per cent for them to win the seat from their Coalition partners.

Both the Conservatives and Liberal Democrats talked about the by-election being a "Two Horse Race". On paper, the figures bore this out, but the real reason for the tagline was that both parties wanted to motivate their own supporters to go out to vote, while driving down the numbers of people voting for Labour or UKIP. Voter turnout at by-elections is traditionally low, usually about half that at a general election. The parties therefore do not spend much time trying to persuade floating voters to come to them because most floating voters don't bother voting. Instead, they seek to motivate as many of their supporters as possible to go to vote so that they have the edge over their opponents. The "Two Horse Race" tactic is a classic by-election ruse.

But the dark horse coming up on the rails was UKIP, led in person by Nigel Farage who spent a lot of time in the seat over the four week campaign. I am told that it was in this by-election campaign that the Conservatives were - for the first time - really worried about UKIP. Their national leadership might affect to despise UKIP and its voters, but the professional staff who were running the campaign in Eastleigh took our efforts very seriously. As the campaign developed, it became increasingly clear that the Tory campaign was not aimed at defeating the LibDems, still less was it targetting Labour. Instead the campaign the Tories ran was all about trying to push UKIP back into a box. You might as well try to put a genie back in a bottle, as the Conservatives were about to find out.

Despite the lack of time to convince voters they deserved their vote, 14 candidates put their names forward for the by-election to be held on February 28, 2013, with only five of them having addresses in the constituency. The list of candidates included the mainstream John O'Farrell for Labour, Maria Hutchings for the Conservatives, Michael Thornton, who hoped to hold on to the seat for the Lib Dems, and Diane James for UKIP.

Michael Walters, the English Democrats' candidate, is a former Lib Dem constituency party chairman who stood in Dover for the party in the 2010 General Election. The party's press release said: "Getting our economy going and beating the recession is a priority for many Eastleigh households who are now experiencing unemployment or having to apply for state benefits to make ends meet.

The Monster Raving Loony William Hill Party candidate was "Howling Laud", real name Alan Hope, who was elected unopposed to Fleet Town Council in 2010. The Wessex Regionalists' Colin Bex said he wanted the ancient region of Wessex, of which Hampshire is a part, to have the right to govern itself. Jim Duggan, from Ireland, was the Peace Party's candidate. Dr Iain MacLennan, a former member of the Green Party, stood for the National Health Action Party. Contesting the seat for the Trade Unionist and Socialist Coalition was Danny Procter, an executive member of the Rail, Maritime and Transport Workers Union.

Labour's candidate, writer and broadcaster John O'Farrell, posted on the party's website: "I've always supported Labour's values. Labour created the NHS after all. I've never been a professional politician. I've had a successful career as a writer and broadcaster, and raised a family with my wife Jackie. Ten years ago I was so concerned about the quality of local schools that I organised with

Nigel Farage talking to the media on the streets of Eastleigh during the 2013 by-election campaign.

other parents to set up a new non-selective state school. My own children went there and I became Chair of the Governors."

Seasoned by-election observers quickly gauged the true level of effort that Labour was going to put into the by-election when the posters started going up. While other parties put the name of their candidate, and sometimes a photo as well, Labour put up only "Vote Labour" posters. Clearly they were saving money by using stock posters taken out of storage.

UKIP's candidate, Diane James, an Independent borough councillor in Ewhurst said she had joined the party in 2010, a year before she stood in two local elections as an Independent. Ms James said: "I do not see an issue with it. It's very much a career choice of my making and has nothing to do with what I am doing in Ewhurst."

Ms James, who used to work for a pharmaceutical company on Eastleigh Business Park, added: "I joined UKIP not only because of their policy on grammar schools, which I benefitted from when I was younger, but because I believe that the UK would be able to thrive outside the EU.

"The response from the people in Eastleigh has been phenomenal – they are fed up with the two parties down there who they feel have let them down. We are aiming to come first – I think there is a very good chance I could win it." She caused some controversy on her first day of campaigning when she called for a temporary halt to immigration to stop Romanians coming to the UK and committing crimes.

There had been some speculation that the party's leader Nigel Farage would stand, however, he decided against, and said: "I stood in Eastleigh back in 1994, famously beating Screaming Lord Sutch by 169 votes. It was UKIP's first electoral fight, and the idea of standing again has its romance. But today UKIP is no longer a small group of idealists. We are becoming a serious player in British politics. As leader I am responsible for what is in the party's best interests.

"In May UKIP will be fighting its greatest yet campaign in the English County Council elections. I will be leading from the front and travelling around the country to bring our message of local democracy and accountability, and to demonstrate why we are the real alternative vote. I also lead a group in the European Parliament united in the belief that Brussels has too much power.

"UKIP continues to grow, and as it does, so the calibre of its candidates improves. We already have a dozen excellent people who have put their names forward to stand as the UKIP candidate in Eastleigh. Whoever is chosen will have my full support, and the support of everyone in the party. We will fight this by-election as hard as we can, and expect to turn what people predict to be a two-way fight into a serious political battle."

The Conservative candidate, Maria Hutchings, was called "the Sarah Palin of the south coast" by one commentator and disagrees with her leader on single-sex marriage and membership of the EU, and has forthright views on immigration and abortion.

The mother of an autistic son, she said she is "not a Tory toff" and has strong local connections. She also contested the seat in the 2010 General Election. A former Labour supporter she came to the public's attention in 2005 when she challenged the then prime minister Tony Blair during a TV debate about the closure of a special school, telling him she was struggling to get her son the support he needed. In 2006 she told the BBC she thought the Conservatives had "snatched the social justice agenda from under the Labour Party's feet".

The man with arguably the most to lose was Michael Thornton, the Lib Dems' candidate. A business and development manager who has lived in Bishopstoke for almost 20 years, he has been a parish and borough councillor since 2007. His election pledges included fighting to protect green spaces from Tory development and gravel extraction; working to bring more jobs and investment to the area and campaigning to cut income tax for local workers.

Starting out as the favourite to win can be a daunting prospect in any election, but in a by-election with the media of the entire country focussing on you it can be terrifying. Mr Thornton seemed to bear the pressure well to start with, but the real pressure was yet to come.

Political commentators predicted that the campaign would test the Coalition with both parties desperate to win and Andrew Rawnsley, writing in The Observer, said the by-election promised to be "short, sharp and potentially brutish". Its importance was highlighted by the fact the leaders of all the main political parties visited to support their candidate at the earliest possible opportunity. According to James Forsyth, writing in The Spectator, UKIP, buoyed by their successes in other recent by-elections, hoped to push Labour into fourth place, and there was a great deal of evidence of support for the party locally.

Nick Clegg wasted no time in showing his support for Mike Thornton and went out on the campaign trail with him on Monday, February 11. He refused to be drawn on the issue of Chris Huhne's shock resignation and told reporters: "Chris Huhne needs to speak for himself. My duty is to make sure the people of Eastleigh aren't without an MP in Westminster for too long. Whatever anyone may think of Chris Huhne, everybody will tell you locally he was an extremely good local MP."

The Conservatives' campaign didn't get off to the best of starts when it was revealed that the description of Eastleigh on Maria Hutchings' website was copied seemingly word for word from Wikipedia. There were also accusations that the Tories were trying to hide Mrs Hutchings, whose views differ from those of her party leader in some key areas, and that her interviews with the national media were being kept to the minimum.

The following day the prime minister was in town and held a "Cameron Direct" event at B&Q's UK headquarters. This had by this date become a standard Conservative Party campaigning tactic. It involved David Cameron appearing live and unscripted in front of an invited audience. Although the Conservative Party is always cagey about how they select the people to invite, it is generally thought that they invite party members and supporters from the constituency involved. The contrast with Nigel Farage's public meetings which are open to everyone could not be clearer.

Giving its opinion on the campaign so far, on Friday, February 15, The Independent ran a piece highlighting the importance of Eastleigh to the Lib Dems and to the outcome of the 2015 General Election, pointing out that the Conservatives are second in 38 of the Lib Dems' 57 seats.

The campaign started to warm up on February 17 when the Lib Dems and the Conservatives accused each other of duplicity over their policy for developments on open spaces. The Lib Dem-run council promised to protect open spaces, but Mr Thornton then voted for more than 1,000 homes on an open space. The Conservative Party chairman Grant Shapps plunged into the argument. After Nick Clegg admitted to local paper the Daily Echo that he wasn't going to apologise for the Lib Dem council's plans to build 5,000 homes on the area's green spaces, Mr Shapps said: "His candidate says 'we have to use green spaces', and yet the Liberal Democrat campaign promises to 'protect our precious green spaces and countryside'. If the Lib Dems have any respect for Eastleigh voters, then Nick Clegg must explain his party's misleading campaign."

As the Coalition parties tore into each other, UKIP was building up its own head of steam and growing in confidence. On February 20 the former Lib Dem mayor of Eastleigh, who had left the party and joined UKIP, urged voters to back Diane James.

Glynn Davies-Dear was a Lib Dem borough councillor for 20 years and a county councillor for 12 years before leaving the party. On UKIP's website he explained his decision. He said: "Why did I leave the Lib Dems? I left in disgust at the lies and the broken promises. The Liberal Democrats no longer care about the people, they only care about themselves.

"I have looked around for a party which still believes in representing the people. The only party that I could find was UKIP. That is why I have given them my support."

Another former Lib Dem, Andy Moore, also joined UKIP. Mr Moore had also served as a Lib Dem councillor on Eastleigh council and said he was: "sick of the self-serving corruption which now riddles the Lib Dem party".

Welcoming them to her campaign, and the party, Diane James said: "I am thrilled to have them on board. UKIP is a growing force in Eastleigh, providing a real alternative. The reaction on the street has been fantastic, we are going to cause a real upset. I am raising the bar and I am not getting personal or dirty. Enough is enough, we want an EU referendum, an end to uncontrolled immigration and integrity in politics."

After attacking the Lib Dems over their plans for development in the constituency, things started to go wrong for the Conservatives when Maria Hutchings declined to appear at a BBC radio hustings on February 21, the same day David Cameron was back in the town. A report in the Guardian said party activists were denying Mrs Hutchings was being hidden away because she is a "loose cannon" after her remarks on gay marriage and state schools. The audience at the hustings booed when it was announced that Ms Hutchings would not be attending.

The BBC reported that Nick Clegg predicted a "two-horse race" between the Coalition partners, while UKIP's leader Nigel Farage said there would be a big swing towards his party.

Countering the claim there was nothing to choose between the Lib Dems and the Conservatives, Nick Clegg stressed the good work of the local Lib Dem council, and said: "There are a lot of people, here in Eastleigh, who recognise what we have done is in the national interest and... whether it is on jobs, on green spaces, on fair taxes, we are the only party with a record of delivery."

However Mr Farage said he thought voters in Eastleigh were "cheesed off" with the Lib Dems and would be voting for his party instead, saying that his party was "coming up on the rails". According to the polls, UKIP's support in Eastleigh had grown from four per cent at the last election, to 21 per cent in the last days of the campaign.

The Daily Telegraph reported that senior Conservatives were already bracing themselves for the possibility they could be forced into third place by UKIP in the by-election, a result that would pile the pressure on Mr Cameron and the chancellor George Osborne. The paper went on to add: "A Lib Dem win would be a major blow for Mr Cameron because the by-election is being held as Mr Clegg's party faces a sexual harassment scandal and follows the resignation of the previous Lib Dem MP, Chris Huhne, after he admitted perverting the course of justice.

"The Conservatives would be unlikely to win the next General Election without winning seats such as Eastleigh."

A senior Conservative source told the paper that winning the seat "has always been a big ask. I suspect it will be quite tight at the top as UKIP is making a late surge. They are picking up the anti-politics vote from all parties in a big way and could even win. It's mid-term and it would be pretty exceptional for us to break through in a by-election when in government — the last time it happened was during the Falklands war."

Speculating on the outcome the day before the polls opened, YouGov's Anthony Wells said: "All the polls have shown the Liberal Democrats and Conservatives quite closely matched, three with leads for the Lib Dems, two with leads for the Conservatives."

According to many political commentators, there was only one real winner in the by-election, and despite the Lib Dems holding on to the seat it wasn't them. The real winners were UKIP, who managed to beat the Conservatives and claim second place, with Labour's John O'Farrell coming fourth.

Mike Thornton retained the seat for the Lib Dems with 13,342 votes, or 32.06 per cent, down 14.5 points compared with the 2010 General Election, while UKIP and its candidate Diane James managed to persuade 11,571 people to vote for them and grabbed 27.8 per cent of the vote. The Conservatives had a fairly torrid night, with Maria Hutchings getting 10,559 votes, or 25.37 per cent, down 13.96 points on 2010. Labour limped home in fourth place with 4,088 votes, or 9.82 per cent, which was up 0.22 per cent on 2010. The remaining candidates polled 2,056 votes, or 4.95 per cent of the vote between them. The turnout was 52.68 per cent.

The rise of UKIP worried Tory MPs, some of whom called for their leader to move to the right. However, as Andrew Grice in the i pointed out, having a right-wing candidate at Eastleigh didn't help the party. Former Conservative leadership challenger, David Davis, disagreed and said: "UKIP are masquerading as the old Tory party. I think there is a lesson there for the Tory leadership about listening to conventional concerns of not so much their membership, but traditional Conservative voters in the provinces." Mr Cameron himself described the result as "disappointing" but continued: "I am confident that at the General Election we can win those people back by demonstrating that we are delivering for everyone who wants to work hard and get on."

The Daily Telegraph's Charles Moore said that Mr Cameron "would be mad to alter his main policy course". He added: "He is a much better leader than his main opponent or his Coalition partner. The more he can lead on the issues that count – the economy and public services in hard times – the better."

The Conservatives had nothing to fear from UKIP and should not read too much into the by-election result, according to Matthew Parris. He commented that the result just proved that UKIP was good at attracting the "to hell with the government" vote. He added:

"Govern well and – when it matters – Eastleigh will notice."

The paper's leader column argued that the Conservatives could not ignore UKIP's appeal to more than a quarter of the voters in Eastleigh, but said the party should not "respond in a shrill voice". The writer said the party had to convince the public "they have the solutions and the vigour to turn the economy around".

UKIP leader Nigel Farage was cock-a-hoop after his party's strong showing and cheekily claimed the Tories split the vote and prevented UKIP from winning. There was differing opinion as to whether Mr Farage would be wishing he had put himself forward as the party's candidate. The leader writer in The Times on March 2, said Mr Farage "must be kicking himself for not standing. He could have been waking up yesterday as the party's first MP." However, writing in the same paper, Matthew Parris said he thought that Mr Farage was simply being realistic and knew that even if he won the Eastleigh seat in the by-election he would have been unlikely to keep hold of it come the General Election.

Speaking after the count, Mr Farage claimed the result was "a massive boost". He added: "People will say it was a protest vote, but who we attracted here were voters who had not voted for 20 years. They are not protest votes." In an interview with Rod Liddle in The Sun he said: "What happened here in Eastleigh was not a freak result. Something is changing. I want UKIP to be seen as the party which represents the ordinary working class voter."

The UKIP candidate Diane James said: "You, Eastleigh, have delivered one humongous political shock."

BBC News' political correspondent Robin Brant said the result was a victory for UKIP. He said: "The march of UKIP continues, Eastleigh was their best-ever election performance. They pushed hard on EU migration and an anti-establishment theme. They were the only ones to put on a significant number of votes. It's clear they are now the new 'protest vote party'. And don't ignore the fact they came close to winning."

Labour had never expected to win the seat and according to Michael White, John O'Farrell came across as a "melancholy kind of clown", he was "likeable and funny, but his heart wasn't in it". The Times believed the party should have tried harder as Eastleigh is exactly the kind of seat they need to try and win if they are to do well in the 2015 General Election.

Perhaps the biggest significance of the result of the Eastleigh by-election was the message it sent to politicians of all persuasions, that the voters struggle to differentiate between them. Writing on the Daily Telegraph's website, Charles Moore said: "Eastleigh brings out something which more and more voters feel...Nigel Farage says that we have three social democrat parties now. There is a bit of truth in that, but I would put it differently. It is not so much that they all think the same thing. It is more that they are all the same sort of people. They all belong to a political elite whose attitudes and careers are pretty different from those of the rest of us."

The Times agreed and said that the vote for UKIP was "first and foremost an expression of revulsion against the political establishment in Westminster". It went on to say that the main parties need to "end this divorce between the political elite and what ordinary people are thinking and saying". It added: "The problem for David Cameron, and indeed all three main leaders, is that they are so trapped in the Westminster bubble that they cannot run as populist, anti-establishment figures."

Robert Winnett, writing for The Daily Telegraph, wondered if the by-election result showed that the established political consensus of recent years has changed. He asked: "Are British voters, like their Italian counterparts, looking for something new, something unlike politics in the past. Is the anti-political mood now holding the balance?"

The Mail online also believed the rise in popularity of UKIP was due to voters wanting to give a "stinging rebuke to the Westminster elite".

A poll by former conservative deputy chairman Lord Ashcroft showed that 83 per cent of people who voted for UKIP at Eastleigh had done so to send a message to the party they normally supported that they were unhappy with their performance, and 75 per cent voted

UKIP as a general protest against the three main parties. The poll also revealed that 22 per cent of people who voted Conservative in the 2010 General Election had switched their allegiance to UKIP in the Eastleigh by-election, with 19 per cent of Lib Dem supporters doing the same. For us a key finding was that 40% of UKIP voters had not voted last time around. We were mobilising and gaining the support of people who had become disengaged from the political process.

And Zac Goldsmith tweeted: "Policies matter, but above all the result reflects an overwhelming view that the main parties lack any kind of authenticity."

I couldn't have put it better myself. But amidst all the general rejoicing in UKIP ranks, there was one little niggle. UKIP had failed to win the same proportion of the postal vote as they had of the main vote at polling stations. This was a recurring theme in UKIP. By-election campaigning had proved to cost the party dear several times. As the number of people voting by post continues to climb, we are going to have to get that one sorted out.

After the by-election result was declared I sent another letter to the press:

As a young child I was fascinated by fossils and picture books of artist's impressions of Dinosaurs. Indeed, I caused much mirth amongst my primary school teachers by telling them I was going to be a Palaeontologist when I grew up.

Unfortunately as the years past reality took hold and my dreams of dinosaur hunting gave way to a reality of a twenty year career in the manufacturing sector. However, my hazy memories of school books about Terrible Lizard still remain.

I remember how the Dinosaurs ruled the planet, seemingly unassailable for many millions of years with the mighty Tyrannosaurus Rex reigning supreme at the top of the food chain. Their reign was cut short by a catastrophic occurrence, possibly an asteroid striking the planet. Unable to adapt and change to the new circumstances the Dinosaurs were replaced by smaller, quicker creatures more suited to the new environment

Nowadays my interests are more of the political sphere but maybe there are some interesting parallels to be drawn. Since the dawning of the modern political scene, giant terrifying creatures have dominated their environment. The Conservative, Liberal and Labour parties have ruled the political world fiercesomely crushing and ultimately devouring all smaller opposition and new parties.

The sheer size and power of these political terrible lizards has made it almost impossible to try and challenge them. Those that have tried as small parties or independents have either been defeated or assimilated. The most effective and powerful of the political dinosaurs has been the Conservative party. Its record of time spent in government always led its supporters to refer to themselves as "the natural party of government" The Tories are the political equivalent of the Tyrannosaurus Rex, right at the top of the food chain, the kings of the jungle !

This is all about to change. In recent years, we have had the political equivalent of the dramatic asteroid strike that wiped out the Dinosaurs. The Financial crisis and the economic recession that has followed have changed everything.

In the difficult times and unstable world we presently live in people are looking for a different approach to politics. They want politicians who are in touch with the realities of the problems that people are encountering and determined to put the needs and requirements of the British people first. Steady as she goes government and a general consensus between the political elite ruling our country is no longer acceptable. The political environment has changed permanently.

The result in Eastleigh is just the latest example of the dinosaurs wobbling. The council elections, Euro elections and finally the Westminster elections of 2015 could see these once all powerful creatures crashing to the ground never to be seen again.

Over the next couple of years we will see the last desperate thrashings of the dinosaurs before their final and ultimate extinction. Maybe some species may survive as smaller, less impressive versions of their former selves, the political version of alligators lurking in Louisiana swamps, like Lib Dems clinging on in Eastleigh while all around them are extinct but the days of the mighty lizards ruling the planet are numbered and the greatest of all of them will fall the furthest.

The ironically named "Modern Conservative Party" is heading for the greatest fall of all. 2015 may well signal their Armageddon. The changes brought about by David Cameron and his " modernisers" have taken the Tories back to the party of Macmillan in the 1950s blended with a very unattractive feeling that they want to pick on the weakest in society to try and prove some kind of economic hawkishness their other policies do not follow through on.

When the General election of 2015 has its results counted the Tory losses may well be catastrophic. They will lose out on millions of votes that they once had an ambition to gain but that have been systematically driven away over the last few years. These votes will have gone to UKIP, a smaller, younger party more in touch with the views of the electorate it is aiming to represent. While UKIP also gains from disenchanted former Labour voters, the Labour party has much less to lose due to the way that the electoral system and boundaries favour them.

David Cameron is on course to be the last ever Conservative leader to inhabit Downing Street. In years to come all that will be left will be fossilised remains of Tory manifestos and the memories of a once great party now rendered obsolete and extinct by an inability to deal with the new political climate.

I know that I have spent a lot of time on these by-elections, but they are important for a number of reasons. The first thing that they show is that the UKIP campaigning machine led by Lisa Duffy has advanced in leaps and bounds since our bad years of 2008. Back then a campaign consisted of the local UKIP members plodding around the streets delivering leaflets about the (undoubted) evils of the EU while the candidate was ignored by the media and Nigel was the only person able to get a journalist to go anywhere other than down the pub.

Now, as I hope I have demonstrated, UKIP runs professional and effective election campaigns. We select candidates who are good performers and hard working campaigners. Our policies are still dominated by Britain's relationship with the EU, but now spread beyond that into other areas that concern voters. In the context of by-elections, we are now listening to our local members to pick up on local issues that we can then campaign on and so attract voters to us. On a more technical level, our leaflets are now better designed and

A UKIP poster displayed in one of the outlying villages during the Eastleigh By-election. By 2012 it was judged that the "UKIP" brand was so well known to the public that it could be used without needing to explain what it stood for. The results from Eastleigh proved this to be the case in triumphant fashion.

written than before, while our media operation has improved out of all recognition. Journalists used to complain that they did not know who to phone to get a UKIP reaction to a story, and when they did get a phone number it went unanswered. Now our media team responds promptly and appropriately.

But perhaps the most important thing to come out of these by-election campaigns was a change in attitude to UKIP by the public. No longer were we the place to dump protest votes, we were now being seen as a political party with an agenda and policies of its own that was worth supporting in its own right. Even more relevant to the future was the fact that the old Tory sneer that "a UKIP vote is a wasted vote" could no longer be sustained. Now we were regularly beating the Tories, and it was a Conservative vote that - in some areas at least - was beginning to look like a wasted vote.

Chapter 6

2013 Trouble in the Shires

Soon after the excitement of the Eastleigh by-election I was made redundant. Ever the positive thinker, I decided to treat being made redundant from my job as an opportunity to throw myself into the UKIP County Council Election Campaign.

Over the past month I have joined campaign teams in areas including Worcestershire, Shropshire, Staffordshire, Derbyshire and Essex. Not only have I managed to add serious mileage to the Etheridge family car but I have shed over two stones in weight!

Everywhere I have been the morale of our UKIP friends and colleagues has been superb. Positive, dynamic campaigning on the local issues that matter to people contrasting sharply with the pathetic mudslinging of the campaign "professionals" at the Conservative party and the masters of hypocritical moral indignation at the Labour party.

Highlights of the campaign have included UKIP activists flying the party flag from the flagpole outside the council buildings in Kidderminster much to the horror of the local Labour party who made an appearance to try and shout our team down. My pleasure at seeing members of the public round on the team in red and support the real people's party, UKIP, was immense.

In Essex, we took over the Chigwell High Street with a street stall and twenty activists. The exciting feeling of the day was added to by a local taxi driver who decided to deck out his taxi with UKIP posters and leaflets then continually drive it up and down the high street making a glorious noise with his horn.

In Derbyshire we went out leafleting and talking to people on their doorsteps. Almost every door was opened by people either curious about or already converted to UKIP.

Shropshire was a day of helping to put vote UKIP signs up on lampposts much to the pleasure of many a passing motorist noisily cheering us on.

Everywhere I have been from the housing estates in Derbyshire to the huge mansions in Worcestershire, from the busy market place in Redditch to the thriving high street in Chigwell the positive attitude of our activists and the interest from the public has made this campaign a real pleasure to be involved in.

It's always important not to get carried away and at no point did I expect UKIP to sweep the board taking hundreds of council seats. I did, however, think that we might make a massive impact and the important thing was that we should use these elections as an important stepping stone towards the real prize of electoral success at the 2015 Westminster elections. I remember telling my wife that I was sure that between now and then there will be many miles of street pounding ahead of us but if we all put the work in not only will activists like me be losing even more weight and improving our health and fitness in the process but we will achieve a dramatic result, changing politics forever and seriously improving the health of our country and its democracy in the process.

One of the issues that the media were keen to talk to UKIP about throughout the build up to the 2013 county elections was that of gay marriage. The background to this issue was that in September 2012 the LibDems had announced at their conference that the government would be bringing forward legislation to legalise marriage between same sex partners. All eyes had then turned to the Conservatives, the larger partner in the Coalition government. David Cameron's office let it be known that he had personally intervened to ensure that this legislation was to be put before Parliament. There was an immediate fuss.

Opinion polls showed the public was fairly evenly balanced on the issue, though as ever the liberal-left elite in London came out heavily in favour of the issue. It was soon clear that the law would be changed, no matter what the people of Britain actually wanted. When it came to a vote in Parliament, most Tory MPs voted against although most of the ministers voted in favour. The legislation was passed.

The media were interested in UKIP's view of the matter. I think that most journalists were after some cheap headlines which would portray UKIP as some sort of swivel-eyed homophobes. The truth, as so often, was different.

Our policy was simply stated, and restated, by Nigel Farage "Civil partnerships represent an entirely common sense way of allowing gay men and women in our country to register in a formal way their longterm commitment to one another and to take advantage of various laws relating to, for example, succession and financial planning in the same way as heterosexual couples. ... Gay marriage is an entirely different thing altogether. ... We are quite sure that, whatever the Government's worthy declaration that it proposes no change to the duties of the Church in relation to the estate of marriage, there will, very soon after the introduction of gay civil marriage, be a challenge in first the domestic courts of England and Wales and then in the European Court of Human Rights alleging that the exclusion of gay people from the right to have a religious ceremony of marriage is unlawful discrimination against them on the grounds of their sexual orientation. We believe that, given the current nature of the European Court of Human Rights' attitude to such matters, there is a very strong likelihood that the Court at Strasbourg will agree that it is an unlawful discrimination on those grounds and order the United Kingdom to introduce laws which will force Churches to marry gay people according to their rites, rituals and customs. This is not a burning issue. It is not a matter which animates the daily discourse of our Nation. There is, apart from a small but noisy minority within the gay community, no strong demand for this. This is therefore not vital to the life and well-being of our Nation and, given the risks attendant upon it, should not be proceeded with."

Journalists had wanted to hear a bigotted rant, so after a while they went away. But the row rumbled on, mostly affecting the Conservative Party. The Tories were split not only in Parliament but in the country. David Cameron had already done much to alienate traditional Conservative supporters, and now he was at it again. The newspapers were soon filled with angry Conservatives denouncing Cameron.

This was all good stuff from UKIP's point of view, but fairly soon we began to notice something else. There was first a trickle and then a flood of activists leaving the Conservative Party and joining UKIP. Having spoken to some of them, it became clear that gay marriage had been the final straw in a long process. For some years they had seen the leadership of the Conservative Party moving away from conservative values. They had stuck with the Tory Party, reasoning that things might change, that Cameron was merely sucking up to the BBC or that one or other right wing MP would put things right. Now they realised that the Conservative Party had stopped being conservative other than in name.

They looked around for a small "c" conservative party that represented their views and saw UKIP.

Now, unlike some of my colleagues I don't think that the gay marriage issue will have a long lasting influence on voting patterns. Most voters have busy lives and think about politics only at election time - and then concentrate on the issues that divide the parties at that point.

However, the gay marriage issue did have a profound influence on UKIP and on our ability to wage effective campaigns. We value all our members and our activists, but we had long recognised that no matter how enthusiastic and hard working activists are, they will achieve little unless they are properly organised by people who know what they are doing. That was what lay behind the drive to professionalise the party.

The types of activists joining us from the Tories over the winter of 2012-13 were the people who had been constituency chairmen, treasurers, secretaries, campaign managers and the like. These were people that UKIP desperately needed and really could use. These were people who knew how to raise the funds for a campaign, how to rally support and get people out on the streets, how best to deploy limited resources, how to deal with journalists and all the other hundred and one things needed to run an effective political campaign. Lisa Duffy is fantastic, but she can't be everywhere.

The gay marriage row was important and will have a long lasting impact on British politics not for its short-lived headlines, but because it removed from the Conservatives an entire swathe of hard-working, talented and knowledgeable local campaigners and gave them to UKIP instead. The actual numbers involved might not be huge, but they were and remain important out of all proportion to the numbers. These are people the Tories could not afford to lose, but which Cameron carelessly alienated and drove away.

UKIP welcomed them with open arms and gave them a home. UKIP really was now living up to the rhetoric and becoming the only truly small "c" conservative party in Britain.

The county council elections that followed in May 2013 were an early sign of the importance of this movement of activists. The impact was patchy as the activists were not yet fully integrated into our campaigning teams, but you could not miss the results.

The elections took place on 2 May and affected 27 counties and 8 unitary authorities in England, plus one in Wales. Since these were local elections the campaigns were dominated by local issues with most candidates talking about park maintenances, potholes in roads and such like. However, the party affiliations of the voters were also important. It was unlikely that a solid Labour voter would vote Conservative no matter how many potholes were in his road. What was more likely was that the voter would stay at home.

These low turn out local elections have traditionally been about motivating people to vote, not changing their minds about which way to vote. A popular, genuinely local candidate loudly backing popular local policies can get his party's supporters up off the sofa and down the road to vote. A lazy candidate from a different area supporting unpopular policies cannot.

When the councils had last been up for election in 2009 the Conservatives had come top with 31% of the vote and 1451 councillors. LibDems had been second with 28% and 484 councillors and Labour third with 23% and 178 councillors. Those elections had been held on the same day as the European Elections, so UKIP had been concentrating on the latter. In any case, this was before the professionalisation of the party had begun. UKIP did not then take local government seriously enough and did not realise the true importance of local elections. We had stood very few candidates in 2009, got such a small % of the vote it did not even register and got 7 councillors elected.

In 2013 things were very different. By now the party understood why local elections are important. For a start they keep our members and activists on their toes. Those working for us on the streets know that they need to identify local issues and campaign on them. They need to identify where our supporters are and encourage them to go out to vote and they need to keep the UKIP flag flying at all times.

From the point of the view of the public, the fact that UKIP stands candidates at local elections demonstrates several things. It shows that we have activists locally. It shows that we care about the local people and their problems with potholes etc, not just the constitutional theory over the EU. It shows that UKIP is made up of people just like them. Perhaps most importantly it gets people into the habit of voting UKIP. If they vote UKIP at European elections and then at local elections the chances are that they will go on to vote UKIP at a general election. Given Britain's first past the post system this is a big ask, but if you don't ask you don't get.

The professionalisation of the party had really taken hold by this date, which combined with the influx of activists from the Conservatives made UKIP a formidably impressive campaigning machine. Nigel, Paul and our other big hitters were touring the media studios in London, then travelling out to the far flung village halls to hold public meetings and address local people. It was all terribly hard work, but it paid off.

When the votes were counted the results were stunning.

The Conservatives had dropped to 25% of the vote (-6%) and to 1116 councillors (-335), The LibDems dropped to 14% (-2%) and 352 councillors (-124). Labour had gone up to 29% (+7%) and 538 councillors (+291). As the main opposition party in Parliament it was not surprising that Labour did well. It was the UKIP result that shocked the commentators. UKIP scored 23% of the vote (+23%) and took 147 seats (+140). It was a staggering triumph for UKIP, and a tremendous blow to Cameron's Conservatives.

The BBC published projected national vote shares, adjusting for which regions are holding local elections and extrapolating to the national situation. These were Labour 29%, Conservatives 25%, UKIP 23% and the Liberal Democrats 14%. The Tories had never been so low, UKIP had never been so high.

Behind these headline figures were some equally amazing local stories. The Conservatives lost control of such solid Tory shires as Cambridgeshire, East Sussex, Gloucestershire, Lincolnshire, Norfolk, Warwickshire and Oxfordshire. Lincolnshire was an especially impressive defeat for the Tories. They lost 24 of their 60 seats, with UKIP taking 16 of those and four others going Independent. In some seats UKIP were achieving electoral swings of 32% or 33% from the Conservatives. It was unheard of. Neither I nor anyone else in UKIP had seen anything like it.

The good news from the polls were followed in June by the appointment of Tim Aker as "Head of Policy". This was a role that, in my opinion, UKIP had long needed. While the main thrust of our commonsense policies was always clear, the detail was sometimes muddled. Policy statements were sometimes made in reaction to some news item and while there was nothing wrong with them, they were occasionally inconsistent with other policies, or lacked a coherent overall drive. Someone was needed to see the big picture. Now we had Tim.

When he was appointed, Tim said "I am delighted to come on board as Head of the UKIP Policy Unit at a time when the party is growing at an incredible rate. We are seeing talented people join the party and contribute to our policy platform. I'm looking forward to coordinating these and ensuring we have a full, common sense manifesto to show the Great British Public that they don't have to settle for the old parties. UKIP is now the voice of opposition on

Tim Aker, UKIP's Head of Policy, speaking to a typical pub meeting in 2013.

Councils up and down the country and I will do my best to make sure we will win the arguments and break into Westminster."

I did not hear him speak until our conference in September 2013 when I was perched high up in Methodist Central Hall, and Tim was striding the stage as if he belonged there. I was impressed. Since then there has been a definite improvement in our overall strategic policies and the way the minutiae tie up with each other.

Tim had previously been with the "Get Britain Out" campaign and with the Taxpayer's Alliance as well as the Freedom Association, so he came to UKIP with a sound track record as a right of centre campaigner and activist with a firm commitment to Brexit.

But things were not all triumph and success for UKIP in 2013, though on balance things were going our way.

There has been a period of time since the start of the UKIP surge when the party and its activists never seem to be out of the media. A remarkable selection of stories have made national headlines. UKIP had certainly added colour and spice to the domestic political scene.

For a radical party led by a charismatic and highly vocal politician to get a lot of publicity is no great surprise. The extent and frequency of the coverage has been totally incredible. There are a combination of factors to blame for this. Of course Nigel Farage would always attract media attention but the "scrutiny" applied to other UKIP members and spokesmen has been fascinating. Many of the people who have hit the national headlines have done so because they were unready for the media attention drawn by the amazing surge in UKIP support. They continued behaving as they did before entering the world of politics and were unprepared for the world of spin that they encountered. Other instances have had altogether more sinister reasons.

Eric Kitson was an example of a man not ready to be in the media limelight. I had met Eric several times and found him to be a pleasant and quite humorous person. He had never said or done anything remotely racist or beyond the pale to my knowledge. He was part of an extremely tough and hard working UKIP team in Wyre Forest, Kidderminster. I had campaigned with the UKIP team in that area several times in the run up to the 2013 County Council elections and when I saw that they had won seats on the council I was delighted.

My delight was short lived however as the local media was covered in stories of racism just days after the elections. Eric had posted highly offensive images on Facebook of anti Islamic nature. Despite the fact that these images had been posted before he was a UKIP candidate it became clear very quickly that the damage to the party was bad but it was fatal to Eric's political career. I was contacted by the BBC and asked to appear on their West Midlands early evening news programme to be interviewed live about the situation. This was a daunting task but I agreed to appear in the hope of limiting the damage to the party concerning the ongoing situation.

I found out about the interview at 9.30am and phoned party

Chairman Steve Crowther to ask for the party line. Unfortunately I could only get an answer phone messaging service on which I duly left a message. I did not get a call back until I was being wired up to appear live on TV. Fortunately Steve gave me the news that Eric was stepping down. This gave me the opportunity to effectively put an end to the story live on air. It was an incredibly nerve wracking experience but the tension was broken when the interviewer raised the issue of Worcestershire UKIP campaigner Richard Delingpole.

Mr Delingpole had launched a deliberate satire of the witch hunt against UKIP members by photoshopping his face onto hundreds of faces surrounding Adolf Hitler. For this issue to be raised showed the desperation of the media to attack us for anything, even having a sense of humour. It was difficult to keep a straight face but I made it through the interview despite my instinct to laugh out loud at the absurdity of the situation.

Mr Kitson resigned as a councillor and ultimately from UKIP. This was a perfect example of a naive man with a very poor sense of humour blundering into the heat of political battle with no idea what to expect and getting very badly burned. His home was raided by police who seized his computer and his health suffered as a result of the stress of the situation. Ultimately a sad story but one the party dealt with in the only way possible. We hoped this would serve as an example to others to be much more careful.

Dean Perks is a good friend of mine. We met through playing cricket at the same club, Claverley in Shropshire. Later I took on a job working for Dean as a paper shuffler and showroom manager for a minimum wage in order to pay the bills while I focussed on my true passion, politics.

Over a period of time I managed to persuade Dean, a former Labour party member, of the importance of the UKIP cause. Not being a man to do things by halves he threw himself into the role of UKIP campaigner with great gusto. When the Coventry branch invited Dean to speak at one of their meetings he took up the opportunity and gave a passionate speech about his political views, a speech that was video taped and put onto social media. Dean was trying to emphasise his opinion that tough sentences deter crime. Unfortunately in trying to do this he mentioned Sharia Law and the practise of cutting off hands. At no point did he suggest or intend to support the concept of Sharia law being applied in this country.

Unfortunately for Dean he and the Dudley & Halesowen branch of UKIP had been targeted by Hope Not Hate. This group, partly financed by Trades Unions and the Labour movement employs people to target political figures that they disagree with. At the time they were organising a campaign known as "Purple Rain" where they targeted UKIP with negative propaganda and smears.

They had contacted Dean through Twitter and told him he was being targeted. In true Black Country fashion he had defied them with words to the effect of 'Bring it on!' They took this challenge to heart. Dean's speech and comments were sent to the Daily Mail and other media outlets where they reported it as a UKIP candidate calling for the introduction of Sharia law. On the evening before the story broke, Hope Not Hate had boasted to Dean via social media that they were finishing his political career before it had even started.

The media storm about this was so intense that I was peppered with phone calls by the media which I dealt with as Dean's branch chairman and did my best to shield him from as he was busy trying to earn a living running his plumbing and home improvements firm. I was unsuccessful in this endeavour when newspaper photographers turned up on Dean's doorstep taking photos and shouting questions. The pinnacle of this event's notoriety arrived when Nigel Farage was interviewed on live TV news and questioned about it. The absurdity of a party leader having to account for a clumsily worded speech by a relatively junior and inexperienced activist was breathtaking. In a superb display of leadership, Nigel launched a staunch display defending Dean. This is the kind of leadership that encourages and inspires great loyalty. The sneaky and cowardly actions of Hope Not Hate are the kind of thing that inspires people to fight on with renewed vigour.

On their website Hope Not Hate claims "HOPE not hate campaigns to counter racism and fascism. HOPE not hate mobilises everyone opposed to the British National Party's (BNP) and English Defence League's (EDL) politics of hate. It was formed in 2004 as a positive antidote to the BNP and has the support of the Daily Mirror, trade unions, celebrities and community groups across the country. At HOPE not hate we want to make sure that people know the full story about who the BNP and EDL are and what they really stand for. The HOPE not hate website aims to do just that, serving the anti-racist and anti-fascist movement and providing up to date news, good practice and analysis."

Unfortunately this is not the limit of their activity. They are running anti UKIP campaigns under the heading "Purple Rain". This campaign seeks to mobilise anti UKIP opinion by highlighting gaffes made by UKIP members and twisting or misrepresenting their words as happened in the Dean Perks case.

There is a very clear political agenda for this organisation and while they claim to be largely against the BNP and EDL they have devoted huge financial resources to a wholly negative campaign against UKIP.

I was proud to support a motion at the UKIP Autumn conference in 2013 calling for the NEC to proscribe Hope Not Hate as an organisation. This means we should ban their members from being members of UKIP. I condemned them as an anti democratic organisation that was determined to destroy UKIP. I'm happy to say the membership supported me and voted for the motion.

Hope Not Hate were involved in another notorious incident. Their emphasis on studying the Dudley & Halesowen branch led them to trawl through the social media sites of the branch and its members. This led to them finding one of the most notorious UKIP related video clips. Godfrey Bloom MEP had been invited to be a guest speaker for the party at an event in the Dudley South constituency as part of our efforts to promote the UKIP cause. We hired a venue in the Kingswinford area called the Kingfisher, a location better known for cabaret events and discos. With Godfrey's reputation for plain speaking we expected an entertaining evening and we certainly were not disappointed.

Godfrey gave a typically entertaining speech which we followed our normal practise of videoing in order to reach a wider audience through social media. There were about 50 people watching the speech including several members of different ethnic groups. Nobody raised an eyebrow at the words or sentiment included in Godfrey's speech and the event passed quite successfully. His speech covered a wide range of UKIP ideas and policies but the area that was later to cause nationwide controversy was when he spoke about foreign aid.

Our good friends at Hope Not Hate once again let us know through Twitter to watch the news the next day as they felt they had put one over on us. Sure enough the next morning the TV news bulletins were full of clips taken from our video of Godfrey's speech where he had referred to foreign aid as sending money to "Bongo Bongo Land" This phrase was being used to suggest racism was the motivation behind speaking against the foreign aid budget. Not for the last time Godfrey's rather old fashioned and extravagant turn of phrase had created trouble for him.

The "Bongo Bongo" incident actually backfired on our opponents with the issue of foreign aid being discussed more than ever before and a very significant amount of public support for the sentiments expressed if not the wording. I had the opportunity to gauge public opinion at first hand in typical UKIP fashion, in the pub. A group of 6 men were talking politics in one of my local pubs unaware of who I was as I sat quietly drinking a pint of Mild at the next table. One of the men stated that he had been a Conservative all of his life but after having heard what Godfrey had said he was switching his allegiance to UKIP. To my delight his 5 friends all agreed. Sometimes it helps to not be politically correct and to just say things as you see them. Of course there is a line and things can be taken too far as Godfrey managed to show just a few months later.

The UKIP Autumn conference of 2013 was held in London. It was the biggest conference yet and the media were in attendance on a grand scale. As a seasoned conference goer I was looking forward to this event and travelled down on the morning with the intention of staying over to enjoy the conference. We were a little late arriving as we had been at a local council by-election count the evening before. Star had been our candidate in the Dudley Borough of Coseley. She achieved a very credible second place driving the Tories into third. As a result of the late evening we were a little late in heading down to the conference the next day.

When we arrived we were met by a good number of friends from the party who kept us talking for a while. Indeed we talked for so long we ended up missing the key note speech by Nigel Farage. Little did we know that the real fireworks were just about to begin.

I was standing in the reception area of the Methodist Central Hall where the conference was being held when suddenly the doors burst open and a huge media scrum came charging through all apparently fascinated by someone who I couldn't quite see, there were so many people around him. Then I caught a glimpse of the journalists' prey, Godfrey Bloom was in the centre of the action trying to push his way through the assorted media. He finally barged his way through a doorway and left his pursuers behind for a short time. A few minutes later the doors burst open again and Mr Bloom re-emerged this time accompanied by burly security staff who cleared a way through the throng for him and bundled him into a car waiting outside.

I pick up most of my political information through the Guido Fawkes political blog and website. I immediately checked my IPhone and sure enough there was the Tweet telling me what had just happened. Apparently Godfrey had struck nuisance and journalist Michael Crick with a conference programme. While I initially sympathised with the desire to wallop Mr Crick, it was obvious that this was a PR problem which became a total disaster when Godfrey's earlier comments that led up to the incident were revealed.

To handle the two incidents that morning one at a time seems the wisest way to approach it as they weren't actually connected despite the fact they happened very close to each other. Godfrey Bloom had been part of an invited group of UKIP supporters in a fringe meeting discussing promoting women and women's issues in UKIP. There had been some banter about women cleaning behind the fridge and when most of the ladies in the room declared they didn't do that Mr Bloom was recorded saying that the room was "full of sluts". That recording then somehow found its way into the hands of the media. Taken in context, it is perfectly apparent that the comments were made using the old fashioned meaning of the term which was used for slovenly or untidy housewives. Taken out of context it is an extremely offensive remark. Not only was Mr Bloom's turn of phrase disappointing but so was the fact that the recording made its way to the media.

Outside the conference area, Michael Crick was reinforcing his reputation as a journalist on the look out for controversy. He had already tried his luck winding up several senior UKIP figures before he hit the jackpot. He confronted Godfrey Bloom with the conference programme and implied that the lack of faces from ethnic minorities featured on it meant that UKIP was somehow not interested in people from ethnic minorities. Mr Bloom took this extremely badly and stormed off, scenting trouble to feature on the evening news, Mr Crick followed him, not a wise move. As they walked Crick continued to bate Godfrey until in a moment of temper, the programme was snatched out of Crick's hands by an enraged Godfrey who then hit him over the head with it. Of course this kind of reaction was just what Crick had wanted and he managed to sabotage all coverage of the UKIP conference through the media and instead the only item covered on the television news on nearly every channel was his showdown with Godfrey.

That evening, UKIP Chairman Steve Crowther announced the party had taken the decision to withdraw the whip from Godfrey Bloom. This was followed up by a speech by Nigel Farage explaining the reasons for the decision, much of which was carried on the national news. The misfortunes of Mr Bloom had effectively removed any positive coverage of the conference from the national media.

These examples of the party and its message suffering from the indiscretions, mistakes and targeting of our membership led to a change of attitude after the London conference. UKIP had always challenged Political Correctness and championed free speech passionately. It was becoming more and more clear that our enemies were using one of our greatest strengths against us. The mood and time was right for a change.

The change in UKIP's approach and a desire for a more professional approach was not universally accepted by the membership or all senior figures. Many people believed that their right to express what they thought in exactly the terms they wanted to was a non-negotiable right and principle. This showed a lack of understanding that when you become a candidate you are a spokesman for your party and you are no longer expressing just your own views but effectively speaking for thousands of other people. Refusal to acknowledge this and to think more carefully in the face of a concerted campaign of smear and ridicule was self indulgent in the extreme. It is perfectly possible to stand by principle while using sober and serious language that is less likely to be manipulated against you or your cause.

The change in approach led to the next major controversy, the selection process for prospective UKIP MPs and MEPs.

Chapter 7

Polling Third, Coming First

A s I write this, the latest national opinion poll to be published has Labour on 39%, Conservatives on 32%, UKIP on 13% and the LibDems on 8%, with the others totalling 9% between them. This picture seems to be fairly stable.

UKIP have been third and scoring between 10% and 15% since the autumn of 2012, before which we were fourth behind the LibDems and were getting between 7% and 11%. One interesting point about these polling figures is that the national opinion polls were showing UKIP on 13% the week before we came second and scored 23% in the local elections. How to explain this?

I think that there are several possible answers to this. It may be that elections record the votes of people who actually bother to go to vote, while opinion polls include everyone. It may be that when people are asked who they vote for in a national opinion poll, they respond with the party they would support at a general election not who they vote for at a local election. Or there may be some other factor at work.

What is clear however, is that UKIP outperform their opinion poll rating at all elections, other than general elections where we usually do badly due to the first past the post system and the national media concentration on Labour and the Tories.

It is not unreasonable to suppose that in the context of a European Election, UKIP can come first even though it is polling third. More than ever before, UKIP must take elections seriously - and that means getting the right candidates.

As part of an overall effort to take a more professional approach

UKIP took on a new system for selecting potential candidates for the Westminster and EU Parliaments from 2013 onwards.

In previous elections, UKIP parliamentary candidates had been selected almost entirely on votes of the membership with a minimal involvement from party officials. This changed when a new system was devised in order to try to improve the quality of candidates.

As I have touched on previously, potential future parliamentary candidates had to first go through an assessment centre where they were tested and examined on their ability to handle the media, deal with public speaking, retain policy and have a good level of general knowledge. Only after they had passed this assessment could a potential candidate apply for a hustings to take on a seat as a prospective parliamentary candidate. This is a comparatively modest change but many of the longer serving members of the party reacted to it almost as if it were the arrival of Big Brother in person.

The selection process for the prospective candidates to be members of the European Parliament was even more controversial. A long time coming after seemingly endless debate, redrafting the process was a fairly simple one consisting of basic background checks, personal interviews and a decisive element of democracy from the party membership. As with the process for Westminster selection, which potential candidates had to have passed before taking part, the system was a long way from the authoritarianism of the old parties and had a huge amount of internal democracy but it was still the subject of great drama and controversy.

The final results for the MEP selection process were dictated by a vote of the membership who were asked to settle the ranking of the prospective candidates for each area, a very important decision in an election settled by Proportional Representation. The internal processes of the party had whittled the candidates down to the correct number for each region before inviting the membership to vote and settle the order.

The West Midlands region of UKIP was no stranger to controversy even before this process began. Having got a very creditable result at the last election in 2009 and returning two MEPs, it was unfortunate that both of the representatives returned had a relationship with the party leadership which was bumpy to say the least. Nikki Sinclaire left UKIP and sat as an independent MEP before eventually forming her own party to compete at the 2014 Euro elections. Mike Nattrass had removed himself from the UKIP group in the European Parliament mid term but had appeared to effect a reconciliation with the party in the months leading up to the candidate selection process.

When the final seven people were selected by the party to contest the Euro elections for UKIP, Mr Nattrass was omitted from the list. This led to a predictably angry response. He attacked Nigel Farage and the party leadership across the media in a series of ill advised and angry outbursts before eventually resigning his membership. These outbursts were so negative and in my view childish that many people who had previously respected Mr Nattrass and had felt sympathy for him following his exclusion from the party list changed their minds and saw the sense of the decision to remove him as a potential UKIP candidate.

Other areas had their share of disappointed candidates but few took the decision in such a churlish manner as Mike Nattrass who turned his back on the activists who had helped him to achieve two terms at the European Parliament and make a very healthy living from it.

The final UKIP Euro election lists across the country showed a great cross section of the British people as our candidates including a very high proportion of women in leading roles giving the lie to the repeated accusations of mysogyny against the party.

The elections of May, 2014, for the European Parliament handed millions of voters in the member states their chance to give their verdict on the direction the EU is taking and its handling of the Eurozone crisis.

The EU is a contentious subject in Britain, with many believing it passes ludicrous laws which other countries ignore while politicians here follow them slavishly. Then there's the issue of immigration and what is seen by a seemingly large proportion of the population as the EU's general interference in this country''s affairs when it should keep its nose out.

The growing popularity of UKIP in both local and national elections has forced the leaders of the three main parties to make their feelings about the EU clear and, some may argue, forced them to make statements more strident than they might have wished.

The campaign for the European elections officially started on September 10, 2013, when the European Parliament launched its awareness and information campaign to try and persuade as many people as possible to vote, and to make people aware of why the elections were important.

The official campaign continues until the newly-elected parliament elected the next European Commission President. Anni Podimata, one of the two vice-presidents responsible for communication, said: "The only way to legitimize and influence EU decision-making is through the European Parliament. There is a perception that EU political decision-taking in the current economic crisis has lacked proper legitimacy. People, EU voters, have the exclusive possibility to determine the political majorities of the Parliament, which will set the course for forging legislation, challenging bad policies and leading the debate in the five years following the elections."

The awareness campaign stressed that the EP is as powerful as any member state's national government as most laws now originate from the EU. Therefore, voters have to be made aware of what is agreed by the EP and how they can influence those decisions.

The campaign had four phases. Phase one ran for a month and had the catchline ACT.REACT.IMPACT. Its aim was to explain the EP's powers and what they mean for people living in the EU, and to emphasise to voters that they could exercise their power to shape the next five years of European policy by voting in May. The campaign's organisers were acutely aware of the growing tide of Euroscepticism, especially in southern European countries.

A specially prepared video was released on YouTube and it said: "In Europe every opinion gets a fair chance. The decisions of the European Parliament are driven by everything that matters to you. You have the power to decide."

Phase two ran from October, 2013, to February, 2014, and

focussed on five key areas - the economy, jobs, quality of life, money and the EU in the world, and included a series of events in European cities.

The election campaign proper, or phase three, started in February, 2014.

The awareness campaign cost 16 million Euros, which works out at 31 Euro cents per person living in the EU, and ran in 28 countries and in 24 languages. A third of its budget was spent on a website and making sure the campaign had a presence on Facebook and Twitter. There was some surprise at the amount of money being spent to establish a presence for the campaign on social media, with some people expressing doubts about its effectiveness in persuading people to vote.

UKIP leader Nigel Farage thought the campaign was a waste of money. He said "You know what? None of it (this campaign) will make any difference at all, because there is now a clear majority of Europeans across all member states who are dissatisfied with this Europe and the direction this European union is going in."

Quite right, if you ask: Have you noticed this campaign going on? No, me neither. Yet another example of how wasteful the EU is with our money and yet another reason why Britain should leave the EU as soon as possible.

Writing for the LSE in May 2013, Simon Hix and Christophe Crombez said the elections would give European citizens the chance, for the first time, to have a direct say on who is named the next Commission president and say yay or nay to greater political and economic integration.

The two academics thought that the main issue in the European elections would be the economic crisis and whether following a policy of austerity was the best way to combat it. They wrote: "Nearly every national election since the onset of the crisis in early 2010 has been fought on the issue of austerity and the consequent relations with the EU. Far from European elections being national elections these days, national elections have started to become European elections."

As for who would be voted the next Commission President, they said that all the European political parties were proposing to field a candidate and that the two parties with the most chance of getting their candidate elected, the centre right party, the EPP, and the centre left PES, have diametrically opposed views on how to tackle the economic crisis. According to Mr Hix and Mr Crombez, the EPP is in favour of keeping austerity policies, while the PES is anti this. Therefore, they argued that voters could decide future European policy by either voting for MEPs from national parties that belonged to either the EPP or the PES according to whether they thought a policy of austerity was working or not. Alternatively, they could reject either option and vote for an MEP who is a member of a Eurosceptic party.

They concluded: "So, in next year's European Parliament elections voters will be presented with several distinct options for the future direction of the EU. The political majority that emerges from the elections will not only determine the policies pursued by the European Parliament, but also the person who will hold the most powerful executive office in the EU machinery – the Commission President. For the first time these could be genuine 'European' elections, the outcome of which will shape European politics for at least the next five years."

Immigration was a major issue for many people in Britain, there were horror stories about hordes of people from Romania and Bulgaria flooding into the country on January 1, 2014, and the impact that would have. On November 27, 2013, the prime minister David Cameron wrote a comment piece in the Financial Times addressing these concerns, possibly in an attempt to counter the growing strength of UKIP, which seemed to be attracting more Tory voters to its ranks than Labour ones.

In his piece, he argued that Britain had always championed the rights of people living behind the old Iron Curtain but that "things had gone wrong". He then went on, perhaps predictably, to blame the former Labour government for what was happening. He wrote that the Labour government had had the chance to exercise "transitional controls", which impose a seven year ban on new citizens coming to

Britain and working here, but had opted out. This was a "monumental mistake" in his opinion.

Mr Cameron then went on to address people's concerns about people coming to Britain purely to live off our welfare state and said his coalition government was "changing the rules so that no one can come to this country and expect to get out-of-work benefits immediately; we will not pay them for the first three months." He went on to add that he was not the only European leader looking for change and said he hoped to work with the interior ministers from Austria, Germany and the Netherlands to "return the concept of free movement to a more sensible basis".

He ended by saying: "The EU needs to change if it is to regain the trust of its peoples", and reiterated that if he was still prime minister after the next election British voters would get the chance to have their say about the country's future in Europe by taking part in a referendum.

Another bugbear many British voters are perceived to have about the EU is what is seen as the excessive red tape. David Cameron also attempted to address this with his "Cut the Red Tape" agenda. This was ridiculed in an article in EUObserver.com in November. It said that Mr Cameron was unlikely to get any other nation to sign up as, although they may agree there was too much red tape, their irritations were not the same as Britain's. It pointed out that one area of red tape Mr Cameron wanted to cut was the issue of increasing maternity leave above 14 weeks, but as most member states in the EU already have more generous maternity leave arrangements this was unlikely to win him any allies.

A major talking point in the early days of the European election campaign was the possibility of holding a referendum in 2017 about Britain's future in Europe, as promised by David Cameron if he was re-elected and mentioned in his FT comment piece, and whether Labour would support it.

In mid-August, 2013, Tom Watson, a former campaign co-ordinator for the Labour party, told The Guardian newspaper that the party should support an early referendum in May, 2014. He also complained that the Labour leadership was allowing the Conservatives to set the agenda on the referendum debate. He said: "Cameron has set the agenda on Europe; he wants a referendum, and if we don't engage with that debate then it won't be on our terms. So I would argue for a referendum next May – get it out the way before the election. That should be Labour's position. Yes to a referendum, and yes to remaining part of Europe."

The shadow work and pensions minister, Ian Austin, had said something similar a month earlier when he argued that the in/out referendum should be held on the same day as voters decided on their MEP. According to the New Statesman, the idea of supporting an early referendum was one the shadow cabinet was discussing in the summer of 2013, but it was fraught with difficulties for the Labour leader, Ed Miliband. His party had made political capital out of David Cameron's rushed agreement to bring forward the draft referendum bill, saying it showed Mr Cameron as a weak leader, so any move by the Labour leadership would have to be at Mr Miliband's choosing to avoid him suffering the same fate.

However, as with many of Mr Austin's pronouncements, this can be written off as a desperate bid to counter the surge of UKIP suppport in Dudley North, where II am the UKIP Parliamentary Candidate who will be opposing him at the next General Election.

The bill for a referendum on Britain's membership of the EU had an interesting background. Cameron and his Eton elite had clearly made a decision to talk about the EU as little as possible. "Stop banging on about Europe", he had famously said some time earlier. However, many Conservative MPs knew that UKIP were making inroads into the Conservative vote. While our success is down to a number of other factors, the EU is obviously one of the more important. The Tory MPs wanted to knock that plank away by seeking to portray themselves and their party as being as Eurosceptic as possible.

Their chance came in the spring of 2013 with the Queen's Speech. The Queen's Speech lays down the outline policies that the government intends to follow over the coming year. It is usually followed by a debate in which government ministers say what wonderful ideas they have, while the opposition counter by saying they are rubbish ideas. It is generally all very predictable and dull.

But in 2013 the debate caught fire when a Conservative MP, John Baron, put down an amendment criticising the Queen's Speech. This was quite unprecedented. Baron's amendment might sound bland, he merely "regretted the absence of mention of a referendum on Britain's membership of the European Union", but in fact it was electrifying stuff. For a government MP to put down an amendment criticising his own government was amazing, for Baron to raise the issue of the EU was stunning.

What followed next was even worse for Cameron. A total of 114 Conservative MPs backed the amendment. Cameron was saved only by the support of Labour. It was humiliating.

A few weeks later, on 13 May, the draw was held among backbench MPs to see who would get the right to introduce a private members bill. The draw was one by Tory James Wharton MP, who promptly announced he was going to introduce a bill to hold a referendum on Britain's membership of the EU. It would be a straight in-out vote. Cameron and the senior Tories bowed to the inevitable and said that they would support the Bill.

The BBC put forward both sides of the case on its website in May. The first question they tackled was: Are there any viable options for Britain leaving the EU?

In the "yes" corner was Nigel Farage, UKIP's leader, who pointed to Norway and Switzerland as two countries that had, and continue to, thrive outside the EU. Both countries have access to the single market, said the BBC, but are not bound by its laws on agriculture, fisheries, justice and home affairs. However, leaving the EU is not that simple, the decision then would be whether to sign bi-lateral treaties with the EU, as the Swiss have done, or join the European Economic Area (EEA), as the Norwegians have done. Or, alternatively, leave the EU completely, leaving Britain free to sign trade treaties with nations around the world.

Opponents to Britain leaving the EU said countries such as

Germany and France would never allow Britain to pick and choose which rules it wanted to follow, and that Norway and Switzerland have to abide by many EU laws without having had any influence in forming them. Indeed, David Cameron said in a speech in 2012: "If we weren't in there helping write the rules they would be written without us...and we wouldn't like the outcome." Additionally, if Britain was to leave the EU, its exports would be subject to EU export tariffs and would still be expected to pass EU production standards.

Another huge consideration is the possible impact on jobs. Those in the leave the EU camp argue that an exit would disentangle small and medium-sized firms from EU rules and create a jobs boom. They point to the fact that half of the UK economy is not linked to the EU but still has to abide by its rules. The Eurosceptic think tank, the Bruges Group, said that leaving the EU would create one million jobs. Those fighting for Britain to stay in the EU argued the complete opposite and said worldwide manufacturers such as the car companies would simply move their production into lower-cost EU countries and that Airbus production would move to France and Germany.

The cost of Britain staying in Europe or leaving was also a debating point. The Treasury has said that the UK paid £8.9bn into the EU budget in 2010/11, out of a total for public spending of £706bn. The sum paid in was about the same as the country spent on unemployment benefits and slightly more than it spent on the railways. The EC, however, said the UK's contribution was £5.85bn.

The better off out campaigners said leaving the EU would save the country billions in fees, hidden tariffs and waste. According to the BBC, UKIP MEP Gerard Batten had worked out that the total cost to the UK of being part of the EU was £77bn a year net (after rebates). Pressure group Business for New Europe said the benefits of being part of the single market far outweigh the costs of being a member, and said the EU was the UK's main trading partner, with 52 per cent of total trade in goods and services being with the Eurozone. They also argued that the UK could lose vital tax revenues if firms dealing with the EU, especially banks, moved to EU member states.

There were also debates about the effect on trade. Those in the get out of Europe camp said leaving would free up the UK to negotiate deals with emerging economies such as China, Singapore, Brazil etc through the World Trade Organisation. However, the BBC quoted Labour's Europe spokesman Emma Reynolds as saying: "The UK is always likely to be better positioned to secure beneficial trade deals as a member of the EU than as an individual and isolated player." This sort of lack of belief in the UK and its future is depressingly recurrent amongs the pro-EU lobby.

The final issue the BBC considered was how Britain's legal system, law-making processes and democratic institutions would be affected by any decision to remain in the EU or leave. Perhaps unsurprisingly, those arguing that Britain would be better off out of the EU said Westminster would have more relevance for voters if the country left the EU. Pro-Europeans argued that Britons benefit from the EU's social protections and employment laws and that would disappear with any move out of the EU. They also said that withdrawing from the European Arrest Warrant would lead to delays in extraditing suspects from other EU countries, and pointed out that the UK has opted out of some EU measures such as the Working Time Directive despite being a member of the EU. This, of course, is ignoring the frighteningly unfair nature of the whole idea. To subject UK citizens to the same standards of law as some other EU countries is entirely unacceptable.

All this talk about Britain leaving the EU should have been good for us in UKIP. After all, it was our main policy plank and had been for years. However, some of my colleagues were concerned that it was the Conservatives who appeared to be making all the running on the issue and getting all the media coverage.

They need not have worried. Since being selected as a UKIP EU candidate I have been out pounding the pavements and have spoken to hundreds of people on this issue. Yes, they like the idea of a referendum and yes they note that it is the Conservatives pushing it in the House of Commons. But again and again I have come across the fact that the voters simply do not trust Cameron on this issue. Quite unprompted by myself, I have found voter after voter hark back to Cameron's "cast iron guarantee" of a referendum on the Lisbon Treaty. "He didn't mean it then," people say. "He does not mean it now." Cameron's duplicity over the EU has come back to haunt him. It couldn't happen to a nicer fellow.

By November 12, 2012, FT.com was reporting that Labour's leadership was coming under pressure from some of the UK's European allies to say whether or not they would hold a referendum on Britain's membership of the EU if they won the next General Election.

According to the report, the issue of whether Britain might leave the EU was one of serious concern for several European countries, including Germany and France, with officials warning the Labour leadership of the pitfalls of holding a referendum. They were aware that David Cameron's pledge to hold one might force Labour into a similar pledge in the hope of holding on to any Eurosceptic Labour voters who might be tempted to defect to UKIP or the Conservatives otherwise.

The FT.com article went on to say: "European powers are particularly worried that it would be harder for the pro-union side to win if it was being led by Labour, rather than the Conservatives.

"Many foreign officials believe that if the Tories were in opposition, they would campaign hard against EU membership, leaving a more difficult task for the 'yes' campaign."

Conversely, the article's author wrote that a yes campaign led by Mr Cameron after a renegotiation of powers between London and the EU would have more chance of success.

The article reported that among the senior Labour figures lobbied were Lord Mandelson, Labour's former business secretary and a prominent pro-European, as well as others in the party known to be close to the leader, Ed Miliband. However, foreign officials were playing their hand carefully as they did not want to be seen as influencing Mr Miliband's decision.

The reaction of the other European powers showed that there was uncertainty about Labour's position on a referendum. While Mr Miliband had not backed David Cameron's calls for a referendum, neither had he said he wouldn't hold one in the future. His failure to come out decisively reflected divisions in Labour's ranks, with the shadow foreign secretary, Douglas Alexander, known to be strongly pro-Europe and anti holding a referendum, while others, including the head of the party's policy review, Jon Cruddas, urging their leader to match the Conservatives' promise. There was also uncertainty about where the shadow chancellor, Ed Balls, stood on the issue. His aides said he backed his leader, but others insisted he was worried that an in/out referendum would create uncertainty that might damage the UK's businesses.

What is quite obvious is that the Labour position on a referendum is likely to shift according to how much support UKIP gains in upcoming elections.

FT.com quoted an official from another European power as saying: "We know it would be deemed as interference if we were to give Labour advice on what to do, but our home government wants us to clarify their position before the next election."

The Liberal Democrats said they were in favour of holding a referendum next time there was any change in Europe that moved power away from Westminster and to Brussels. However, both Ed Miliband and Nick Clegg were under pressure from some in their parties to support David Cameron's promise so that they weren't seen as being unwilling to allow British voters the chance to have their say on the future of the UK in Europe.

The bill calling for a referendum on the UK's membership of the EU in 2017 was finally approved by MPs on November 29, 2013, despite attempts by both the Conservative's coalition partners, the Lib Dems, and Labour to delay it.

James Wharton, the MP behind the bill, said the decision was a "significant" milestone in the attempt to allow voters to have their say on the issue. David Cameron had strongly supported the bill, believing that the country needed to renegotiate the terms of its EU membership and that the British public had to give any new deal their backing. However, by the time of the vote, the Lib Dem leader, Nick Clegg, and Ed Miliband had both come out and said that they thought any uncertainty caused by holding a referendum would be bad for business.

I see Mr Wharton and his Bill as little more than a useful tool for Mr Cameron and his pro-EU lobby supporters so that they can repeat the mindless mantra "Vote Tory for a Referendum" whenever UKIP is raised. But like the previous "cast iron guarantee" of a referendum on the Lisbon Treaty, it is essentially meaningless.

Labour MPs had tried to hinder the bill's progress through the House of Commons by speaking at length to try and make sure it ran out of time, but to no avail. At one point during the debate, Labour MP Mike Gapes spoke for 38 minutes and called the bill "a pig in a poke". He condemned it because it was built on a belief that the terms of the UK's membership of the EU would be renegotiated and that might never happen. He added: "This bill is a disgrace."

UKIP wanted the referendum to be held before May's European elections because it said that any decision to hold a referendum could be overturned by a future government. The party's deputy leader Paul Nuttall said: "The people of Britain are wise to this nonsense now and will view today's vote as the cowardly buck passing that it amounts to."

Shortly after the vote, the i newspaper ran a front page story on the results of a survey by ICM Research on the attitudes of young people to the EU.

A poll conducted in Germany, France, Poland and the UK and reported in the Guardian at the beginning of December, showed that British voters are more anti-Europe than their European counterparts. The poll, by Opinium, reported that just 26 per cent of the British people surveyed regarded the EU as a "good thing" overall, compared with 62 per cent in Poland, 55 per cent in Germany and 36 per cent in France.

The survey, of 5,000 people, also showed that the majority of those asked were against giving Britain a special deal to make sure they remained in Europe with low support for British membership among their continental cousins. When asked about the UK's contribution to the EU, nine per cent of Germans and 15 per cent of French people

The UKIP European Campaign in the West Midlands kicks off in the first week of February with a street walkabout in Birmingham.

said they thought the UK had a positive influence on the EU, although the Poles were slightly less harsh, with 33 per cent saying the UK had a positive effect. Only 16 per cent of Germans and 26 per cent of the French people polled were in favour of allowing the British government to negotiate a special deal to stay in the EU.

The poll's results prompted Nick Clegg to say his party's candidates in the European elections would be representing a party that wanted to stay in Europe. He told the paper: "Everybody knows the EU needs reform. But simply carping from the sidelines and flirting with exit undermines British leadership in the EU, fails to deliver reform and leaves Britain increasingly isolated. The debate about Europe is no longer about who is for or against reform – everybody agrees on that – it is between those who believe we can lead in the EU and those who want to head for the exit.

"That's why next year's elections will be so important: the Liberal Democrats will be the leading party of in."

Labour's former Europe minister Peter Hain said the poll showed it was time for pro-Europeans to wake up and fight, arguing that if the Conservatives won the next election Britain would leave the EU and that would be "an utter disaster for British jobs, prosperity and influence in the world". He went on to say that the poll's findings also said it was time for the "Brussels Bubble" to realise it was totally out of touch with voters.

Interestingly, the poll showed that voters across the Channel shared British voters' fears about immigration, with 59 per cent of French people polled saying the EU's immigration policies have a negative effect, compared with 64 per cent of British voters. However, the British were not totally against everything the EU does. Just over half said they thought the EU's free movement rules are good for tourism and there was a big thumbs up for free trade, with almost half saying they believed the lack of customs controls and tariffs on goods and services was a plus.

The Guardian quoted UKIP leader, Nigel Farage, as saying: "This is a fascinating and comprehensive study into the relative relationships between countries within and about the EU. We, on these islands, due to our history as a globally trading nation, feel much more at home with our cousins in the Anglosphere than we do with our friends on the continent."

As the year drew to a close and fears about a potential influx into the UK of Romanian and Bulgarian jobseekers on January 1, 2014 – the true extent of which may take years to be wholly appreciated – intensified, the coalition government rushed through a series of measures aimed at quelling those fears. The new rules included: EU jobseekers having to wait three months before they are entitled to apply for out of work benefits; only those people who can supply compelling evidence that they will be able to find work being entitled to continue claiming benefits after six months; no new EU jobseeker would be able to claim housing benefit; any EU migrant found sleeping rough or begging would be deported and refused re-entrance for a year unless they could convince the authorities they had a job, and all EU immigrants would be asked about their English language skills and about what they had done to try and find a job before they entered the country.

So far as many in UKIP are concerned, all of this is no better than window dressing. A typical example of Cameron's Tories talking tough but not dealing with the real core issues. This fact is being increasingly noticed by the public who are becoming wise to professional politicians who mouth the right words, but fail to deliver.

As an example of what is now expected from a UKIP European Candidate I give here my diary for a week chosen at random from recent activity.

> *Monday 17th February*
> *Phone calls start from 9am*
> *Jim Carver rang concerned about the arrangements for the fundraising lunch planned for Friday at Worcester Cricket club. We are keen to ask the press along but want to make sure that we only invite people who will give us at least a reasonably fair hearing.*
> *Several other callers rang one after the other to discuss administrational matters around the West Midlands. None of the calls were particularly urgent but when taken one after another they took up virtually the whole morning.*
> *Emails sent out to promote fundraising events around the region*
> *Public meeting tonight with Neil Hamilton in Harborne, Birmingham. Approximately 100 people crammed into a*

church hall. Less than half of the people there were known UKIP members or supporters. Several people in the crowd told us they were abandoning the Conservative party at least for the Euro elections as they felt the time was right for a jolt to the political system.

People from every different section of society and many different ethnicities all united in their desire for change. A truly exciting evening with a great atmosphere and a revolutionary fervour in the room.

Tuesday 18th February

Constant stream of phone calls from 9am onwards. One of the hardest parts of our campaign is combining the duties and concerns of a Regional Organiser with those of a candidate. Unfortunately we have no choice but to do this due to the behaviour of our previous MEPs who left the party and took their funding and most of their staff with them. We are now left with a totally volunteer team trying to cover a huge area with next to no funds but a very large supply of enthusiasm and good will.

Leaflets dropped in with volunteer campaigners in the Handsworth area of Birmingham

UKIP West Midlands Regional Committee meeting on the evening. Largely positive feedback from the regions. A couple of branches needing extra support and guidance are being helped.

Main issue is the need for fundraisers to raise money to fight an effective campaign. Several events planned around the region but much more needed

Wednesday 19th February

Meeting in Wolverhampton at the Great Western pub at lunch time with chairmen of Wolverhampton and South Staffs branches. Plans under way for a major public meeting, a leafleting drive and at least one fundraising evening

Evening meeting of Dudley & Halesowen Branch. A serious chance of winning council seats here so plans need to be formalised and actioned. The meeting was fantastic. The branch has a full slate of council candidates for May and have begun going out saturating wards in groups of ten or more working under the title of "The hit squad" and delivering large numbers of leaflets. There was a real feeling of excitement and revolutionary fervour. Over 30 people in attendance and a spontaneous collection to help with the Euro election campaign raised £200.

Thursday 20th February
A quieter day today. Leaflets delivered to volunteers in Birmingham. Many of these volunteers are not party members or even very political but they want to do their bit for change.

A lunch with our volunteer press officer to organise a series of press releases across the region. We are having good results from targeting local issues across the West Midlands.

Yet more phone calls and Emails on administration issues.

By 2014, UKIP's campaigning methods had come on in leaps and bounds. This image appeared as a website advert for a public meeting with Nigel Farage on Tyneside.

Friday 21st February

A big day of fundraising and campaigning today

The first event was at Worcester Cricket Club where Neil Hamilton was the guest speaker talking to a room full of local members, supporters and business men. While it was a successful event it was still sad to look out at the most beautiful cricket ground in the country and see it under approximately 4 foot of water.

On the evening we travelled over to Telford where a UKIP Farming and country matters event was hosted by Jill Seymour and Christopher Gill with guest speaker Stuart Agnew MEP.

After a long day we had raised some money and made some new friends.

I checked my phone at the end of the day and found half a dozen voice mails from calls I hadn't been able to take all chasing me about matters of administration. I responded to all of them by Email when I returned home in the hope that people will get used to communicating by Email rather than the time consuming phone calls that are making it very difficult to fit in all of the campaigning we need to do.

Finance continues to be the biggest challenge we face in our campaign but we are confident we can overcome any obstacles with the huge wave of public support we have behind us

Weekend

Very pleased that an interview I gave to the local press calling for a straight In/Out referendum on the EU has made it into the local press as part of a piece featuring well known local political figures.

I have managed to have a weekend free from UKIP activity and spending some time with the family. It may be my last for a while.

Monday 24th February

After a day of dealing with various Emails and phone calls from across the region I attended a meeting of the Wolverhampton branch of UKIP on the evening. Despite a relatively low turnout we gained two new members. One an ex Labour activist and the other a lady originally from Lithuania who believes our immigration system is too open to abuse. This really is a wind of change.

Then came the excitement of the televised debates between Nigel Farage and Nick Clegg, leader of the LibDems and Deputy Prime Minister. I was not lucky enough to get tickets for the show, so I watched the debates live on TV like millions of others. What I saw was fascinating.

The journalists on the TV had brought in a variety of pundits and politicians to comment in the run up to the debate - predicting what subjects would be covered, how the two leaders were likely to behave, soundbites to watch out for and that sort of thing. Rather amusingly everyone who was brought in to comment sided with Clegg, with only one or two making lukewarm noises about Nigel.

Now, I am not saying that this was a deliberate attempt at bias by the companies involved. Any such attempt would be unprofessional and very likely against the rules on balance that broadcast media need to adhere to. No, what was happening was that all the pundits, journalists and politicians came from the same sort of background, worked inside the Westminster Bubble and had a similarly cosmpolitan and urban outlook on life.

Without exception they concentrated on issues of interest to the urban elite and predicted that the smooth Clegg with his much greater experience of television and of televised debates would have the edge over Nigel.

Then the debate took place. Now, I know I am biased but I would have given Nigel the lead by quite a wide margin. He spoke well in everyday language, while Clegg used Westminster jargon. Nigel knew statistics when he needed them to make a point, but did not get bogged down in reams of facts and figures like Clegg. And I thought Nigel came across as more relaxed and engaging than the stiff and formal Clegg. But as I said I am biased.

So, it would seem, are the journalists. When the debates finished they hurried to the microphone to say how Clegg had clearly got the better of Nigel in the debates. I could not see it myself and was just starting to think I was hopeless at judging these things when the results of a poll organised by YouGov for the Sun newspaper. That said that the public had given the victory to Nigel by 57% to 36%, it was a convincing win.

You could almost hear the head scratching among the inhabitants of the Westminster Bubble. Clegg had performed well by their criteria, he was one of them, speaking their language, trotting out their facts and explaining their views in clear and concise terms. But he had lost. And he had lost to a bloke who - if early accounts are true - had come to the debates on foot from the local pub where he had been having a beer with some mates. Clegg, by contrast, had come by ministerial limousine having been prepared for the encounter by a host of clever media gurus and media consultants.

The journalists and politicians gathered in the TV studios did not understand how Farage had won. Well, I understood and if you have read this book carefully you should understand as well.

Conclusions

As a youngster, I loved the American Marvel Comics. These comics gave us Superheroes like Captain America, Spiderman, The Hulk and Iron Man. This was much to my parents' chagrin as they were much more keen on telling me tales of great English heroes both historically factual and mythical.

I gained an appreciation of Robin Hood, Boudicca, Drake and of course the greatest of them all King Arthur. As I have grown older the tales of King Arthur have grown more and more meaningful to me. This is a hero who didn't just fight the bad guys, he created a better world for his people and stood for honour, justice and decency.

This subject has been stirred in my mind by a recent news story. This story suggested that Arthur's round table wasn't actually a table but a Roman Amphitheatre near Chester.

To my mind, the basic story of Arthur is of a man who displayed truly noble characteristics. He was known to be brave in the face of his enemies, generous to those who needed help, honest in his dealings and unquestionably acted with his people's best interests at heart at all times. He was not perfect of course, he was still a man, with human weaknesses. For example he wasn't best pleased when his finest Knight seduced his wife! So we are not talking about an immaculate Saint but we are talking about a man who displayed the virtue and honour of a true Gentleman.

In order to be a gentleman or to follow the role model set out in the Arthurian legends you do not need to be wealthy or born an aristocrat. The virtues he showed are free of financial charge to gain and are attainable by all of us. To coin a phrase we will all have heard from our mothers "good manners cost nothing" I suggest that good conduct and a sense of chivalry are equally lacking in financial cost.

Of course, not everyone can achieve the knightly virtue shown by the original gallants of Camelot. While these virtues are not attached to financial cost they do bring a cost of another sort. They require people to be honest in their dealings and to be able to resist the temptation of personal gain through low dealings. Very few people have led a blame free life and I would be the first to admit to having often behaved in ways that could have been classed as dishonourable in my past, personal life.

Where I do think people have an absolute duty to be entirely honourable is in "public life" Anybody who seeks to be a politician and hold office, no matter how lowly , should be prepared to conduct themselves in an entirely honourable fashion. If your general conduct is honourable, people will be prepared to accept that whilst they may not always agree with your policies or the way you implement them, you are doing what you genuinely believe to be right.

Modern day leaders and politicians in this country are seen as the very antithesis of the Arthurian model. Years of blatant dishonesty and manipulation entirely aimed at personal gain by a minority of those in public life have created an almost entirely cynical electorate. People believe that all politicians are "in it for themselves" or change dramatically once they achieve office and all too often they are proved right. Unfortunately this atmosphere leads to even the earnest and genuine members of our political establishment being dealt with harshly and given no benefit of the doubt. A genuine error or slip of judgement is magnified into something much more sinister under the scrutiny of a cynical media and public.

The United Kingdom finds itself at very low ebb. We have been involved in unpopular wars. The economy is shattered. Our people seem to have lost their sense of identity and national purpose. If ever we had a need for great leaders and heroes now is the time, because unless we do something to change the current trend our nation is heading towards an irreparable fall from grace and power.

The legend of King Arthur says that he and his knights are sleeping. Waiting for a time when their country needs them to return. We certainly need a return of their spirit in order to bring back a sense of British pride and patriotism. Our leaders and by leaders I mean everyone from the town councillor to the Prime Minister, should seek to display the characteristics I earlier defined as embodying the spirit of King Arthur. It doesn't matter if they have the occasional problem in their personal life, I don't believe we want Saints as our representatives. What we do need are people who we know are entirely motivated by love of country and the wellbeing of its citizens.

Politicians can come up with all of the slogans they like, we will not believe they are "working for you" or think we are "all in this together" until we believe more in the people uttering these slogans.

We have so much to be proud of in this country, not all of it based in distant history. We have wonderful musicians, sports stars and entertainers. Our National Health Service is extremely modern. We have a good level of law and order. Education is free to all. Our scientists are amongst the best in the world. Our armed forces are probably the most technically skilled in the world.

Couple these achievements with many I may have missed and the fact that our history is filled with great achievements and you see a country that should be holding its head very high .Indeed the British Empire was only rivalled by that of Rome for greatness in the history of the planet. As well as all of this, our literature and art has been and in some cases still is, the envy of the world.

This great country with its wonderful people deserves better leadership. If we can find a generation of leaders who will run their public lives in the inspiring, honest style that Arthur represents, I have no doubt that they can inspire this nation and its citizens to a future even more magnificent than its glorious past.

I have put forward my vision for how our nation can be revitalised. I have an optimistic assessment of our country and its people; I truly believe we have it in us to make a full recovery.

I am often told that there is no way these changes will ever happen and no way that a radical like me will ever be able to make a difference. My aims and hopes for our country are dismissed as fantasy and dreams. Well as someone once said, "you may say I'm a dreamer but I'm not the only one"

There are many people in our country who share my dream of a new Britain surging forward as an independent, powerful nation populated by dynamic, positive people. The biggest difficulty we have got is the feeling of national depression and resignation to permanent national decline. Britain can be great again, we can do it!

That is why I am a member of UKIP. That is why I am standing for election as a UKIP candidate. That is why I am proud to have played a small part in:

The Rise of UKIP

General Election Results

Year	Candidates	Votes	Seats	Deposits saved	% national vote	% Votes in seats fought
1992	17	4,383	0	0	0.01	0.53
1997	194	106,028	0	1	0.34	1.06
2001	428	390,575	0	6	1.48	2.16
2005	496	603,298	0	38	2.2	2.8
2010	572	919,546		99	3.1	3.45

European Election Results

Year	Votes	% national vote	Seats won	Position
1994	150,251	1	0	8th
1999	696,057	7	3	4th
2004	2,650,768	16	12	3rd
2009	2,498,226	17	13	2nd

Local Election Results

Year	% national vote	Seats won	Change from when last fought
2005	not given	0	-1
2006	not given	3	0
2007	not given	5	-1
2008	not given	8	+3
2009	not given	7	+7
2010	not given	9	-4
2011	not given	7	+7
2013	23	169	+147

Acknowledgements

All photos and illustrations by the author, except:
Campaign bus 2004, Ian Roberts; Nigel Farage 2008, Euro Realist Newsletter; PCC 2012 Stephen West, Stephen West; Exeter ukip poster 2009, Lewis Clarke; Nigel Farage 2014, DAVID ILIFF. License: CC-BY-SA 3.0; Nigel Farage and tv camera, Stephen West; Nigel Farage at UKIP Basingstoke office opening 2012, Stephen West; Gerard Batten at London Mayoral Count, Secretlondon; Campaigning in Newport 2012, Stephen West; Roger Knapman, Roger Knapman; Paul Nuttall, Paul Nuttal